Becoming-Woman

Edited by

Sandra Buckley

Michael Hardt

Brian Massumi

THEORY OUT OF BOUNDS

...UNCONTAINED

BY

THE

DISCIPLINES,

INSUBORDINATE

PRACTICES OF RESISTANCE

...Inventing,

excessively,

in the between...

PROCESSES

OF

HYBRIDIZATION

Becoming-Woman

Camilla
Griggers

Theory out of Bounds   *Volume 8*

University of Minnesota Press

Minneapolis • London

Chapter 2 first appeared in Laura Doan, ed., *The Lesbian Postmodern*,
copyright 1994 by Columbia University Press.
Reprinted with permission of the publishers.

Published by the University of Minnesota Press
111 Third Avenue South, Suite 290
Minneapolis, MN 55401-2520
Printed in the United States of America on acid-free paper

LIBRARY OF CONGRESS CATALOGING-IN-PUBLICATION DATA
Becoming-woman / Camilla Griggers.
p.   cm. — (Theory out of bounds ; v. 8)
Includes bibliographical references and index.
ISBN 0-8166-2716-9 (hc)
ISBN 0-8166-2717-7 (pb)
1. Feminist theory — United States.   2. Femininity (Psychology)
3. White women — United States.   4. Lesbianism — United States.
I. Griggers, Camilla.   II. Series.
HQ1190.B42   1996
305.42'0973 — dc20
96-31404

For my grandmother
Gregoria Benolirao
Manila, 1913–1942

Contents

Preface

This book is about what woman is becoming in U.S. culture at the end of the twentieth century. She is becoming predatory (in 1991, Aileen Wuornos became America's first female "serial killer");[1] she is becoming depredatory (by 1985, U.S. women were aborting 1.5 million fetuses per year).[2] She is becoming militarized (in 1990, Linda Bray became America's first woman in combat).[3] She has synthetically altered personalities (6 million Americans were on the neurochemical Prozac by 1993 — the majority women);[4] she has prosthetically altered body parts (some 2 million American women had received breast implants by 1994).[5] She has had her biological functions exchanged on the open market (in 1992, there were 4,000 surrogate births in New York state alone).[6] She is becoming publicly lesbian (lesbian chic is in vogue in fashion). She is becoming despotic (black men dragging the face of white femininity are the U.S. media's darlings, while images of white women are exported around the globe for mass consumption). And she is becoming at the cellular level a toxic site, ripe for neoplasty (by the end of the millennium, an estimated one in three American women will be diagnosed with some form of cancer).[7]

My premise in this book is that woman is an abstract-machine concretely produced by late-twentieth-century technologies and capital. Her forms of expression are determined by optical and electronic media, psychopharmacology, the war machine, the chemical industry, plastics technology, bioscience. In this sense, the abstract-machine of femininity could not be more material. She is the gaze smiling at you from the page; she is the voice calling to you in electronic transmission. She is the one who turns her head indifferently from you to stare into the camera eye, or into the radar screen as she runs bombing missions over the desert. In private, she cannot help vomiting what she has consumed into the toilet. Her womb is a politics, as is her face.

Gatekeeper to both current expendable income levels and future national demographics, she will produce the next generation of voting blocks, laboring and fighting bodies, and consumer markets. Thus her becomings must pass through a body appropriated by New Reproductive Technologies even as her reproductive rights are fought over by invested institutions of power, including the abstract Justice system, neo-right "family values" coalitions, the American Medical Association and American Law Institute, and, most recently, the pharmaceutical industry in the form of the synthetic abortifacient pill RU-486.

I have taken the concept of abstract-machine from the later writings of Gilles Deleuze and Félix Guattari in the two volumes of *Capitalism and Schizophrenia*, in which they define abstract-machine as a conceptual formation that, when activated, legitimizes not only an overcoding of signifiers and meanings but also specific assemblages of organic and nonorganic properties by channeling the molecular flows of signs and matter. In this sense, femininity is an overcoded, abstract faciality mapped over the surface of actual bodies. This does not mean those material bodies don't signify, because they constantly do. But often, they can only signify in the form of depression, psychotic breaks, bipolar disorder, posttraumatic stress syndrome, victimization, outbursts of rage and violent revenge, anorexia or bulimia, or malignant neoplasties—that is, as breakdowns in the machinic production of the feminine as an intelligible body of signs. And these breakdowns in turn mobilize the machinic workings of various social institutions that channel, mediate, and regulate—not to mention diagnose, arrest, and turn a profit off of—her arational and adestinal becomings, just as the mental health industry is called into action precisely when the abstract-machine of rational cognition and behavior breaks down. Even in her flights of madness and (dys)functionality, she has provided biopsychiatry with one of the largest growth markets in the United States at a time of national low-growth economics (Prozac earned Eli Lilly $1.2 billion in profits in 1993).[8] Each becoming, each transformational encounter with regimes of signs that constitute her public intelligibility, each failure of her social being (because she is both the icon of social privilege and its sacrificial victim), is the scene of emergence and constraint, market development and social investment, and, often enough, social violence.

To take up the challenge of becoming-woman is to come into the transformational potential of these legacies constituting contemporary feminine social experiences, and to do so without nostalgia for a lost identity of the past or illusion about a future, ideal destiny to come. To become-woman is to enter the micropolitics of becoming-molecular, to pragmatically enter the flows of matter and signs that have made up the turbulent and proliferating histories of the feminine in contemporary U.S. culture, and to understand the delimited yet real possibilities for transformation that those histories afford.[9]

There are no easy passages. The call-to-being proffered women as their share of an Enlightenment legacy of individual identity brings with it a politics of shifting seductions and investments. Between the 1970s and 1990s, the substance of expression of a woman's "full" civil rights as an individual citizen within the public sphere shifted from the right to oversee her own reproductive functions (as constitutive of the distinction between public and private space) to the right to hold combat positions in the war-machine. As Massumi notes in *A User's Guide to Capitalism and Schizophrenia*, to become is to come out from such a call to identity and *survive*.

In writing a book on becoming-woman, I hope to contribute to the immense theoretical project of reformulating our understanding of, and inventing new conceptualizations of, the process of social subjectivization under late capitalism, a project begun in the writings of Deleuze and Guattari. My goal is to advance the theoretical exchange already taking place in the United States between a pragmatically oriented feminism and Deleuze and Guattari's particular strain of post-Lacanian, poststructuralist cultural theory. Following the methodological injunction against psychoanalysis articulated in *Anti-Oedipus*, I have privileged "schizoid" becomings over Oedipal being as one viable feminist strategy for sign production because, as Deleuze and Guattari put it, "schizos don't mistake the buzz of the crowd for Daddy's voice." In the chapters that follow, there are many, many wolves.

My Filipina-American mother was introduced to the seductions of white femininity via Betty Grable movies exported to Manila (the obvious source of Imelda Marcos's symptomatic clothes fetish); she entered the United States as part of the traffic in Asian women that accompanied every U.S. military operation in the Pacific. For me, a second-generation Filipina-American, the face of white femininity has always been both a seduction and a horror, and its despotic forms are as clear to me as its forms of victimization. Airbrushed, PhotoShopped, screened, and electrified, the identity of woman exported around the globe and repetitively reproduced at home is the face of class and race privilege. All minoritarian becomings must (de)face the face of her despotism, just as the well-known African-American transvestite RuPaul had to mime her signifying and subjectifying imperialism, passing *as* her before s/he could pass through her privileged body of signs into the public sphere. Woman is the gatekeeper to minoritarian passings, standing vigilance in movie theaters, in fashion magazines, and on the television screens of commodified desires. And at the same time, inside the American family and its "values," she is the battered, the raped, the incested, and the murdered. In any sacrificial economy, there are two types of scapegoat. The liminal, marginalized body living at the edges of the socius and the body closest and dearest to the seat of power — the body bearing the most privileged and precious signifier. She is both.

Because my goal in this book is to facilitate an exchange between feminist cultural studies and the poststructuralist writings of Deleuze and Guattari, the chapters that follow are not structured as critiques. I leave the task of critique to others, some of the work of which has already been started by Alice Jardine in *Gynesis.* Instead, I have followed the lead of Rosi Braidotti and Elizabeth Grosz, inquiring into the uses of Deleuze and Guattari's work for feminism.[10] Further, I have structured the chapters as a series of experiments and explorations of what knowledge-effects the philosophical concept of *becoming*, rather than being, can produce in regard to contemporary U.S. women and the social forces that are shaping their histories and their futures.[11] In addition, while several arguments are made in the book, I have designed each section not as an argument so much as a textual space and temporality in which meanings can be allowed to proliferate and resonate. Because there is nothing like the horror of staring into a face and realizing gradually that it is not human, my goal is to assist the reader not only in an intellectual knowledge of becoming-woman but also in an affective understanding of the implications of that knowledge for her own lived memories and emotions. In this way, I hope to counter the effects of the schizophrenic disconnection between language, affect, and the body that so characterizes living in contemporary culture.

Many women, both academics and nonacademics, have touched specific sections of this book, each leaving her own mark on the effect of the entire assemblage. I am particularly grateful to Avital Ronell, both for her intellectual support and for the model of interdisciplinary experimentation for which her writing stands. In addition, Elspeth Probyn provided editorial advice at an early stage of the manuscript that shaped the final outcome. Judith Halberstam guided the final version of chapter 5. Alida de Paz provided engaging intellectual debate, moral support, and food for the soul in the early days of conception of this project, and for several summers of research and writing. Audrey Kuenstler constantly challenged me to allow affect to have a voice in theory, and helped me understand the relations between af-fect and violence in the lesbian community. For many late-night conversations on how best to apply the theoretical works of Deleuze and Guattari to pragmatic femi-nist issues, I thank Lesley Gamble. I am also indebted to Miranda Monkhorst as much for spiritual support in moments of self-doubt as for several timely discussions in the areas of nonlinear dynamics and biochemistry that helped to shape the early drafts of chapter 6. Though there is no way to adequately mark her influence on my writ-ing, I want to thank Gail Shepherd for her patient, insightful, and rigorous editorial advice. Every theorist should know a poet who thinks a pen a scalpel. I also often turned to Lisa Frank in moments of difficulty in the writing process, and always re-ceived from her the most astute edits, from which I always found a way to go on. Fi-nally, much of the writing that makes up this book began as discussions with students in graduate seminars I have taught, and I dare say this book would never have be-come in the way it did without those (molecular) exchanges.

Pittsburgh, 1996

O N E

The Despotic Face of
White Femininity

The Face Is a Politics

Let's start with her face. A composition of dark lines on a light surface, the public face of white femininity is a highly regulated, mass-produced organization of signifiers and interpretations. Make a dark line with a hole in it on a white screen, add a black dot next to painted lips, and it is her face that appears. Her face makes signifiers accumulate meanings. Her face makes signifieds resonate consciousness. Her face constitutes social being, class status, race privilege, *fashion*.

        In this 1950 fashion photograph for *Vogue*, Erwin Blumenfeld aestheticized the face of white femininity, making visible the fundamental elements of the abstract-machine organizing discrete social subjectivities through the face. As Blumenfeld's photograph demonstrates, the face is produced when two elementary mechanisms—screen and percept—come together to make what Deleuze and Guattari call "the white wall/black hole system" of faciality (1987, 167). The white screen of signification provides a ground for the appearance of the signifier. The black slash of subjectification cuts across the white plane, constituting a vortex of consciousness on the ground of signification (168). The *eye* holds a crucial and fragile position in this visual regime of signs. Through the eye, signification and subjectification are integrated by the face and mapped over the entire head and body. Obviously produced by the mechanical gaze of a camera lens and photoprocessing, the

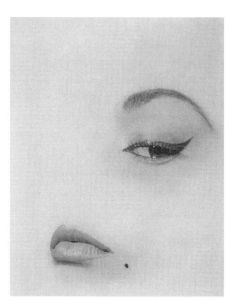

Erwin Blumenfeld. Courtesy *Vogue*. Copyright 1950 (renewed
1978) by the Condé Nast Publications, Inc.

photograph calls the viewer to identify with the technology itself, its frame, or some
piece of its assembled (macro) landscape, such as mascara and eyeliner, foundation
makeup, lipstick, or lighting. This mechanically produced gaze constituting the face
of white femininity in fashion is inhuman—as inhuman as the face that stares at you
blankly from the photograph. Nothing could be more clear.

      While Blumenfeld was aestheticizing the face and its elemen-
tary functions in the early 1950s for a post–World War II audience still reveling in a
fantasy of national plenitude signed in the face of fashionable white femininity, Harry
Harlow was busy subjecting the faciality machine to the rigors of scientific method.
In his experiments with artificial surrogate mothers in captive monkey communities,
Harlow scientifically verified the fundamental mechanisms of faciality while acting
out technoscience's desire to appropriate maternal functions within an inorganic
socius. Whereas the proprioceptive body is all volume, the face is all *surface*. Substitute wire mesh for the mother's body, stretch a white cloth around it to constitute a
ground for the signifier, add the black cut of subjectivity (a simulation of the leaking
black orifices of consciousness—ears, eyes, mouth, nostrils).[1] In other words, substitute the inorganic face constituted in technology for the organic body. Both re-
markably and horrifically, baby monkeys continued to respond to surrogate faciality

Inorganic faciality substituted for the organic body. Harry
Harlow's surrogate mother experiments. Courtesy Harlow
Primate Laboratory, University of Wisconsin.

despite the fact that there was nothing organic about it. Still, many of them became
anxiety-ridden, disturbed, and, in Harlow's own descriptions, protopathological.[2]

Whatever conclusions Harlow presented in his research reports,
his surrogate-mother experiments proved above all else that faciality is not simply a
matter of maternal identification. It is a question of technology, of a machinic operation of signs. Not only in the instance of the surrogate mother but also in the case
of the fashion photograph, the face is a machinic assemblage of signs territorializing the plane of visual perception within which the mother's face once appeared as
percept, and which once indexed the proximity of the maternal breast (169). Faciality is this machinic assemblage.

The face is not a signifier of an individuated consciousness but
"a signifying mechanism," a network of interpretations organizing a zone of acceptable expressions of the signifier and acceptable conductions of meanings to signs and
of signs to social subjects (168, 176). Subjectivization *is* facialization, a social process
that begins with the production of binary facial units. That face, is it a man's or a
woman's? Wealthy or working class? Fashionably seductive or in poor taste? There
are not two faces, as Deleuze and Guattari are careful to point out, but one face with
binary aspects—a *biunivocalization* stabilizing a unitary privilege that truncates mul-

1946: Before and after faces of a lobotomized woman. From
Freeman and Watts's *Psychosurgery in the Treatment of
Mental Disorders*, 1950. Courtesy of Charles C. Thomas,
Publisher, Springfield, Illinois.

tiplicitous proliferation. Is she white or colored? Straight or lesbian?[3] Sane or mad?
The face will tell. And if she is something else entirely, the social process of facialization will capture her in one aspect of a categorical binary or its other, even if it has
to do so by making a third term. In this way, "borderline personality disorder" contains within a general and pervasive psychopathology anything exceeding the biunivocalization of normalcy as psychosis—the (other) face of rational cognition and
behavior.

Faciality is a system of signs and a system of subjectivization
that not only assembles signifiers and signifieds into biunivocal facial units, but also
regulates possible degrees of divergence between those units and any number of nonconforming singularities. Biunivocalization is accompanied by a process of selection
(177). Does the individual face conform to socially intelligible limits? Are its deviations intelligible? Does it *pass*? Faciality serves a policing function. Moreover, if the
face can proliferate redundantly while expanding its borders into new territories,
it is by definition "despotic."[4] Its imperialism is materialized in the mimetic demand
it places on anything that comes into its expansionist sign-flow.

Nowhere is the despotic face of white femininity made more visible than in black drag, in which African-American queer men make a spectacle of the white woman's majoritarian regime of signs. Outrageous, the black drag queen plays with the abstract-machine of faciality in one of its primary functions—regulating the limits of perception of signifiers and subjectivities. The most famous African-American drag queen of the 1990s, RuPaul entered the mass-mediated public sphere as a blond-white-woman assemblage, that is, as a composite of gendered, classed, and racialized signifiers. RuPaul *was* lipstick; blond hair bleached to an artificial purity; foundation makeup masking all skin blemishes and constituting the white wall of signification; mascara accentuating the black hole of consciousness; low-cut evening wear for the cleavage of desire; gowns, heels, and jewelry for class status. And RuPaul passed. S/he passed into the public eye. S/he became a name, s/he became a popular star, s/he became fashion and publicity. The power of the face. S/he signed a record contract. Certainly no one could mistake RuPaul for a white woman. Yet even in drag her face drew its circle of power. The seductive power of the screen icon. The power of class and race operating through the face of the fashion model. It attracted significance. It lured signifiers. It seduced viewers and financial backers. It gave RuPaul the cultural capital he did not have as a young African-American queer from a broken home growing up in the streets of San Diego (Yarbrough). In drag, RuPaul became a public icon. He became a *face*.

RuPaul as queen of American drag certainly tested the limits of public (im)perceptibility of minoritarian subjectivities, yet the black transvestite could only become perceptible to a broadcast public gaze, could only have access to a public sphere now constituted by the mass media, by taking on the face of white femininity. Not a referential signifier for an individual identity, faciality is a system of signs organizing a zone of perceptibility and intelligibility for the socially constructed subject. As such, the face neutralizes, channels, and polices minoritarian forms and substances of expression. For this reason, Deleuze and Guattari write that "the face is a politics," because it is on the face that the limits and thresholds determining (im)proper conductions among signs and meanings are charted (181). Faciality is the "substance of expression of the formal redundancy of the signifier, the overcoding of the signifier, the limit of the deterritorialization of signs" in the process of social subjectification (115). The face is where the majoritarian establishes itself as such by reterritorializing minoritarian becomings. The face is where the minoritarian deterritorializes the signifier for its own even as it is caught in becoming majoritarian, thus it is "the Icon proper of the signifying regime, the reterritorialization internal to the system" (115).[5]

RuPaul as a woman. Photo by Greg Gorman. Courtesy of
The Advocate.

Once s/he was well established in the media as a popular icon,
RuPaul came out on the cover of *The Advocate* after the Stonewall 25 celebration in
1994 as a "man." Caught in the apparatus of biunivocalization, RuPaul's media face
was quickly reconfigured along traditional and familiar lines. In the cover story
photograph, RuPaul takes the pose of Angry Young Black Man for photographer
Greg Gorman. Looking away from the camera, he gazes into a distant horizon of self-
willed fate and bears the tropes of masculinity, complete with plaid work shirt, as
well as he did those of the feminine. Square-jawed and square-shouldered, with
mustache and goatee, RuPaul contemplates the burden of his future as a queer black
singer and performer out from under the seduction and the containment of his drag
face.

While this image, anchored by the caption "The Man behind
the Mask," suggests that the *real* RuPaul lay behind the mask of white femininity,
we know that this RuPaul is neither more nor less real than the RuPaul who became
herself in blond wig and blemishless foundation. RuPaul is produced in the zone
between two limit-faces. The face is not separable from the organization of signs
that constitutes it in the social; "the mask does not hide the face, it *is* the face" (115).

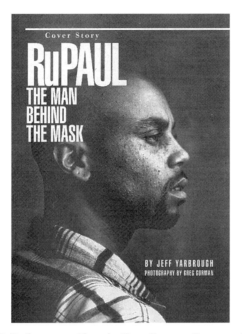

RuPaul as a man. Photo by Greg Gorman. Courtesy of
The Advocate.

And when the subject takes it on, and when it takes on the subject, s/he is constituted within the limits of its overcoding system. These limits designate "the penultimate marking a necessary rebeginning," the point at which the system of signs will reproduce itself, and the reterritorializations internal to that system (biunivocalization, selection, etc.) (438). This is not to suggest that RuPaul cannot change her face, because s/he did and s/he can, but there is no getting beyond faciality. One can even slip by the last limit to pass through a threshold, "the ultimate marking an inevitable change," and land in an entirely different landscape of signs — into madness, for example, or martyrdom, alcoholism, or criminality (438). Passing through such a threshold, however, does not end faciality, does not free the subject from the social restraints of the face; it merely initiates different limits.

The lesbian's passage into mainstream representation in the United States in the early 1990s fashion trend of "lesbian chic" further exemplifies the working of threshold transformation and the instantiation of new limits. To appear in public, the lesbian must pass, like RuPaul, through the face of the White Woman and her landscape of commodified signs. Here the regime of signs constituting the despotic face of white femininity regulates and channels minoritarian be-

Apparatus of capture-lesbian chic. Cover of *Elle*, June 1991.
(*Elle* editorial staff refused permission to reproduce.)

comings on their way toward the public spaces wherein circulate the signs that constitute the majoritarian. This process of transformation has carried lesbianism through a threshold of change. But in passing from the repressed and negatively valued spaces of "the closet" and the subterranean becomings of after-hours bar culture to fashion's broadcast medium, the lesbian must enter a social and semiotic space rigidly striated by race and class privilege. Deviations of color and homoeroticism can become intelligible to the fashion system, but only if those deviations can be contained by a mimetic limit as sameness, not difference.

The cover of the June 1991 issue of *Elle* epitomizes this apparatus of capture in regard to lesbian chic.[6] To be lesbian in public is permissible and acceptable, even desirable, if that becoming can pass as fashion, that is, pass as recognizable, mimetic repetitions of the commodified signifier. How is it that we know so well that it is not the woman on the right who is becoming into the darkness of her mimetic double, but the woman on the left who is becoming white in a landscape of whiteness against which "color" can "bust out on the big screen"? Here lesbian chic works as an apparatus of capture for the signifiers of both sexual and racial difference. One can undergo a process of effacement, one can even defacialize, but one cannot escape facialization. One cannot flee the landscape of signs in which the face appears as the "pure formal redundancy of the signifier" (115).

Faciality as a system of overcoding includes not only the surface of signs mapped over the head and body but the landscape in which the face appears and the objects in that landscape (181). The face *is* its landscape and objects—*haute couture*, lipstick, lighting, and foundation. Observation laboratory, cage, and research funding. Psychiatric institution, psychopharmacology, and mental health. Commercial break, electronic transmission, and switchable programming—any number of framing and projection devices, not to mention production methods and distribution systems. It is not only the body that is facialized, but all its surroundings and all the objects in those surroundings. When one is facialized, one takes on not only the face but the face's delivery and distribution systems, its transportation and mediation mechanisms, and its means of production.

Becoming-woman implies becoming-molecular, fleeing facialization, defacializing, and even losing face in a politics played out between the perceptible and the imperceptible. But as RuPaul and lesbian chic demonstrate, becoming-woman also implies being facialized, undergoing facialization, and having one's becomings captured by the despotic face of white femininity.

The Social Function of the Despotic Signifier

The despotic face is an abstract-machine organizing concrete semiotic procedures for drawing signs and subjects toward a center that expands even as it closes off its boundaries. That is, the despotic signifier is a mechanism of reterritorialization. As such, the despotic face functions as an apparatus of capture for deterritorialized particle signs and subterranean becomings. Its overcodings protect the regime of signs against destabilizing asignifications from within and the intrusions of foreign signs from without. Because it works by installing a redundant signifier at the centers of many different expanding territories, it is an imperialist system of signs. Its redundancy is its semiotic imperialism, the means by which it perpetually recharges the signified and reterritorializes the subject toward the Face of the White Man—and his counterpart, his screen, his other, and his symptom—the Face of the White Woman (182).[7]

Deleuze and Guattari describe the despotic signifier as the "limit of the system's deterritorialization" and the "supreme signifier presenting as both lack and excess" (117). The despotic signifier is the signifier in its "pure redundancy," emptied of specific meaning and therefore excessive in its signification (114). Her face—it means nothing and everything at one and the same time. Here its airbrushed

The redundant, despotic signifier posing as "Nadja Auermann."
Harper's Bazaar, September 1994. Courtesy of *Harper's Bazaar*.

surface marks the limit of desire, of commodification, of value, of seduction — the limit of signification itself. Its lack and excess together stabilize the unstable signified, anchor it publicly to a redundant signifier through repetition and overcoding while veiling its expansionist imperialism as value. This imperial despotic regime of signs requires "deception in the regulation of interpretations" yet "publicness of the facialized center" (117). A public deception, the face of white femininity is the form of substance of the despotic signifier in its bourgeois incarnation. An expression of power suitable for consumption by the masses, the radiating expansion of the despotic regime of signs applies not only to the fashion system, but to "all subjected arborescent hierarchical, centered groups: political parties, literary movements, psychoanalytic associations, families, conjugal units, etc." (116). Its workings can be seen wherever an expansionist reterritorialization reproduces itself in radiating units organized by a central signifier.

Contemporary expressions of despotic faciality bear vestiges of a feudal economy of representation deterritorialized by capitalism for mass consumption. If the feudal economy of representation consisted of "the paranoid face of the despot (God) in the signifying center of the temple," the modern economy of mechanical reproduction consists of the face of the White Woman in the signifying center of Madison Avenue, where the despotic face is feminized, democratized, mass-reproduced and exported abroad (116). Where there was once the priest at the center of the temple recharging the Signified "by transforming it into signifier," there are now the designers of Madison Avenue at the center of the marketplace recharging the Signified as class status, racial traits, and nationalist characteristics by mass-producing the face of white femininity (116).

In its capitalist forms of expression, the despotic face tended toward democratization, feminization, and mechanical reproduction simultaneously. The face of the White Woman nicely serves a dual function within a political economy of the sign organized by commodity logic: it recharges the social value of race and class privilege while providing a commodity for mass consumption and export. By the end of the Second World War, the bourgeois form of despotic faciality born in the face of classed, white femininity was well established in Hollywood and the fashion industry, where the faciality of the White Woman fueled popular and profitable domestic and export industries. Her face expanded semiotic and commercial territories, signed and regulated discrete social bodies and social status, and legitimized dominant social relations by overcoding the signified and mass-producing the signifier in a landscape of technoprogress, commodification, and hypermediation.

In this 1951 fashion photograph for American *Vogue*, the face of white femininity gives social meaning to the landscape of modernization, progress, and technologization that surrounds it—even as that landscape gives the face of white femininity its full social significance. Framed at the center of a twentieth-century train of progress, travel, and leisure, the White Woman rationalizes race and class privilege, market expansion, modernization, excessive expenditure, and mediated consumption. Her faciality reigns over the entire landscape of modernity's signs, its logic of the commodity, and its world of consumable objects, transportation technologies, and redundant public mediations. Through mechanical reproduction and mass distribution, the despotic face of the White Woman in fashion continually exteriorized its substance of expression, radiating outward and extending the borders of its expansive landscape.

Today the export of U.S. fashion journals to Asia provides a pointed example of the expansionist movement characteristic of this faciality. *Elle* magazine, for example, monthly exports the face of white femininity to Japan, where Anglo-European racial traits stand in striking contrast to the faces of the Japanese women who make up *Elle Japon*'s market. While Japanese fashion journals feature Japanese women on their covers and in their photographic layouts and advertise-

Constantin Joffé. Courtesy of *Vogue*. Copyright 1951
(renewed 1979) by the Condé Nast Publications, Inc.

ments, U.S. fashion journals marketed to Japan typically feature American and European models, making Occidental racial traits an integral feature of exported fashion. The U.S. fashion system sells the faciality of the White Woman as a commodity to Japan, including the landscape of signs in which her face takes on its full significance—designer fashions, the expansive spaces of wealth, the accoutrements of class privilege, the poses of spectacle and domination, the value of technology, and the mediated sign as acceptable object for consumption. This is the signifier in its pure redundancy, emptied of all significance except that of its own privilege and repetition, and offered up for mass consumption to foreign markets. If a bathing suit is sold in the process, it is only one object-sign in a vast landscape that desires to territorialize the face of Japanese femininity for its own while capitalizing on the face of the White Woman as a national product.

Territorializing Japanese femininity was a formally stated U.S. military and cultural strategy during the Allied occupation of Japan between 1945 and 1952. The Civil Information and Education Section of the occupation government carried out pre- and postproduction film censorship in order to "pursue the principles of the Potsdam Declaration," that is, to "democratize" postwar Japan (Hirano 5–6). Postproduction censorship was also carried out from 1946 to 1949 by the Civil Censorship Detachment—a military intelligence agency (6). Central to the proj-

Elle Japon. June 20, 1994. Courtesy of *Elle Japon.*

ect of democratization was reprogramming — refacializing the Japanese Woman. As in the United States, it was the woman who would become the substance of expression of the signifier of bourgeois democracy, at the same time that she became the commodity form of that signifier. The shift from industrial militarization to postwar democratization would be carried out in part through her face, which would anchor a whole landscape of "democratic" (i.e., nonfeudal, noncommunistic, and commodified) relations and objects.

This social process of refacialization was epitomized in the contemporary contention over the Japanese woman's public kiss. Kissing on-screen was recommended by the Civil Information and Education Section in spite of the fact that public kissing was never an accepted practice in Japanese culture, and that eroticized representations in film were widely seen during the prewar and war years as signs of Western decadence (154). As if to penetrate the orifice of Japanese consciousness through the mouth of the Woman, the occupation censor boards were successful in prying open the mouth of the Japanese screen star — refacialized as an individual bourgeois subject — to receive the American kiss (149). The result was that, while the effects of the atomic bomb, incendiary bombing, and "fraternization" between occupation troops with their pockets full of yen and Japanese women were forbidden representations for public consumption in movie theaters during the occupation, the eroticization of the face of Japanese femininity—which went hand in hand with her democratization—was systematically engineered (54–59).

If U.S. audiences did not see the effects of the atomic bomb in Japan in the late 1940s, 1950s, and 1960s because Japanese newsreel footage of Hiroshima and Nagasaki was held as classified material by the U.S. government for a quarter of a century, they did see the effects of cold war militarism in Vietnam in the 1960s.[8] The despotic face of white femininity at home in fashion eventually found its haunting other on the Pacific front. American fashion had entered the international fashion scene during World War II, when the occupation of France and the effects of total war brought the Paris fashion industry to an abrupt halt, allowing both New York City and Los Angeles to compete as major producers of the face and landscape of classed white femininity (Devlin 124). By 1968, American fashion was alive and thriving, expanding its sales to international markets even as photojournalism from the war zone in Southeast Asia began to infiltrate the evening news, weekly news journals, and the daily papers, exposing another face of femininity—the face of the Vietnamese woman as sacrificial victim. The despotic face would know its other in the face of the sacrifice.

Ronald Haeberle, the army photographer assigned to Charlie Company during the My Lai massacre on March 16, 1968, estimated that U.S. troops killed at least 150 unarmed civilian Vietnamese in four hours—three-quarters of whom were women and children. Later estimates went as high as 400 or 500 dead—all witnesses agreeing that the vast majority were women and children. Haeberle's personal slides of the massacre provided army investigators with a criminal case, and provided the press with a sensational, though short-lived, front-page story that vied for a time with the second moon landing of 1969 for media coverage (Bilton 241). Only one U.S. soldier, Lieutenant William Calley, was convicted of any crime for the My Lai murders, and his sentence of life imprisonment with hard labor was lifted within three days by Nixon's presidential intervention pending appeal. Calley was paroled after three years (2). Testimony gathered during the investigation verified that rapes and random violences toward Vietnamese villagers were common experiences in Charlie Company long before My Lai (81).

The social function of the sacrifice is to keep violences appropriately contained within the margins of the majoritarian social body. That Charlie Company itself also constituted a sacrificial body was the horror that the My Lai massacre served to screen. Only three weeks before My Lai, Charlie Company was directed by its own superiors into a minefield laid by South Korean troops—allies of the United States. The company suffered horrific casualties. Witnesses reported that one soldier was split in half vertically from his crotch up to his chest when he stepped on a land mine. When the company medic tried to retrieve the body, he detonated a second land mine, reducing the corpse to bits of steaming flesh. The medic, who was the only trained medical professional at the site, suffered a nervous breakdown on the scene (Bilton 84). My Lai was a desperate and successful attempt by Charlie Company to reconstitute the sacrificial signifier—at any cost—on the appropriate(d) body of an "enemy" other. Other faces from the landscape of the sacrifice in Southeast Asia, such as those of children deformed by the U.S. military's use of the defoliant Agent Orange, never made the front-page news.

As combat photographers and photojournalists imaged the war zone and its aftermath in Vietnam in the late 1960s and early 1970s, the fashion industry continued to produce its monthly quota of hypermediated images of class and race privilege for public consumption. The social function of the despotic signifier in its late-modern substance of expression is to recharge the social value of a majoritarian regime of signs while veiling the violences in its border zones with consumable representations of bourgeois identity. Fashion has always served this representational function by producing a consumable face for white femininity, as has the Hollywood cinema. From the end of World War II through the 1960s, the U.S. cinema was screening nostalgic representations of America's frontier past to audiences via the popular genre of "the western," while the actual U.S. frontier had moved to Southeast Asia for the Korean and Vietnam wars. The early western screened the imperialist desire behind U.S. policy in Southeast Asia—and its violence—with consumable, nostalgic representations of a glorified national past. John Ford's *She Wore a Yellow Ribbon* (1949), starring John Wayne as a calvary officer in a righteous war against indigenous peoples, is a classic example of the genre in its heyday. In the late 1950s, the western's expansive landscapes were "modernized" with the new technology of cinemascope in a failed attempt to compete with broadcast television. The genre declined in the 1960s as images from the continuing war zone in the Pacific front infiltrated the media—its end marked perhaps by Arthur Penn's *Little Big Man* in 1970 in which the horrific, bloody battle scene depicting Custer's maniacal campaign against the Sioux presents a thinly veiled representation of the My Lai massacre. While the cinema could preview the face of the sacrifice for mass audiences, however, she would rarely enter fashion's privileged location at the center of production of a consumable feminine faciality. Fashion would remain the most pure form of despotic signification.

In contrast to the despotic signifier, the social function of the scapegoat is to contain everything that escapes despotic signification—"everything

The defacement of the sacrifice. Vietnamese children fleeing
napalm, 1972. By permission of AP/Wide World Photos.

unable to recharge the signifier at its center and everything that spills off the outer-
most center" of its radiating, expansive territory (121). Whereas the despotic face
incarnates difference as sameness, the face of the sacrifice incarnates difference as
difference, so that it can be marked with a negative value or overtly antiproduced
(116). The sacrificial counterbody is then made into "the body of the tortured or ex-
cluded" (115). It is transformed by excessive expenditure of resources and life, and
by the violent reterritorialization of signs and spaces. Scapegoating is a function of
the despotic signifier—the process by which it contains particle signs and becomings in excess of and beyond the reign of despotic signification (116). The body of
the sacrifice by definition is perpetually *losing face*—undergoing a process of effacement, a trial of humiliation, exile, or victimization in a militarized zone transformed
by violent reterritorialization (115).

Despotic faciality veils the landscape of the sacrifice, a violent
landscape of expansionist reterritorialization that its regime of signs requires and
rationalizes. Screening the sacrifice with consumable images of bourgeois identity
is the despotic signifier's representational function. On the level of subjectification,
despotic signification channels social violences toward appropriate social bodies, designates appropriate effacements, and, when necessary, antiproduces inappropriate becomings. It reterritorializes subjects and landscapes of alterity—reducing them to
sacrificial values or to simulacra of sameness. Its radiating and proliferating centers
of power attract deterritorialized particle signs, capturing them within the limits of
intelligibility and familiarity that it both prescribes and legitimates.

The White Woman as the embodiment of the abstract-machine
of despotic faciality holds a precarious position within this economy of signs, however. The feminine is itself the minoritarian substance of expression within the ma-

Isabella Rossellini as a victim of domestic violence. *Blue Velvet*,
directed by David Lynch, 1986.

joritarian biunivocalization of man/woman. Thus, while the White Woman provided
the consumable face of democratized and feminized bourgeois identity that would
help screen violences toward minoritarian social bodies reterritorialized into the face
of the sacrifice under expansionist capitalism, she was also often required to become
that face, to take it on and have it take her on in a trial of effacement. If her face did
not hold together as an intelligible and consumable organization of signs and meanings, if she exceeded the limits of her own face — that is, deterritorialized the despotic
regime of signs which her face incarnated, she might herself take on the negative
value of the scapegoat by which inappropriate becomings are blocked. Wherever her
becomings exceed the limit of the signifier, she is in danger of violent reterritorialization. Wherever her unstable significations deterritorialize the signifying sign to
the degree that they exceed the limits of its system, her becomings must be blocked
or captured. She must undergo the humiliation of the scapegoat in order to contain
through negative valuation the threat of "subterranean becomings" that "exceed the
excess of the signifier or pass beneath it" (116). Unlike fashion, the cinema could
convey both the despotic face of white femininity and its double — the face of the
scapegoat as sacrificial victim.

Here Isabella Rossellini, daughter of classic Hollywood screen
icon Ingrid Bergman, plays the sacrificial body in David Lynch's *Blue Velvet* (1986).
In this role, in which she plays a mother terrorized by domestic violence, she appears
naked and beaten. Whereas in Lancôme advertisements for which Rossellini was paid
some $2 million per year, one does not see her asymmetrical breasts and surgically
repaired, scoliotic back — the organic body glossed with makeup, lighting, airbrushed
photography, and electronic image manipulation in the landscape of fashion and
advertising — that body can appear in the modern cinema.[9] The appearance of the

sacrifice marks a discursive limit distinguishing the cinema from both fashion and advertising.[10]

Lines of Flight and Apparatuses of Capture: Deterritorializations of Despotic Faciality

Classic Hollywood in the studio years from the 1930s through the 1950s was in its own right a center for the mass production of a consumable classed feminine faciality. It produced the despotic signifier as feminine screen star, manifested not only in film but also in publicity. The face of Garbo. The face of Ingrid Bergman. The face of Monroe. The landscape of designer fashion imported to the silver screen. The coifed hair, the alcohol, the cigarettes, the latest electronic appliances as the accoutrements of class status in an endless flow of projected social images.

But in the cinema, the White Woman also took on the face of the sacrifice. The appearance of both the sacrificial and despotic signifier in one plane of representation is always potentially destabilizing, unless those destabilizations are channeled through a proper sacrificial body. In the popular genre of film noir, the proper sacrifice was the White Woman herself, transformed into a victim whose signifier could absorb the potential chaos of signs and meanings that surrounded her. The "black widow" of the noir tradition embodied dangerous deterritorializations of feminine despotic faciality. These deterritorializations were signed in her independence as an urban single woman from the claims of family and clan, her disregard for codes of conduct and law, and her threat of deviant sexualities, whether in the form of an uncontained heterosexuality or as a potential auto- or homoeroticism, or the homoeroticism of the viewing audience in regard to her screen face. At the same time, she would bear the cost of those deterritorializations. Her face would capture runaway becomings and absorb destabilizing significations. Her body would bear not only despotic facialization but also the despot's counterbody—the face of the sacrifice. In *The Maltese Falcon*, the classic detective film of the pre–World War II period produced in 1931 and again in 1941 with Humphrey Bogart, the femme fatale, in spite of all her attractions and seductions, had to be criminalized and finally arrested before the narrative could come to adequate closure.

Traversed by the historical flows of time beyond the frame of individual filmic narratives, the face of the feminine screen icon suffered from any number of interior deterritorializations—flights into alcoholism, for example, in the case of Joan Crawford playing herself in *Humoresque* (1946), or the public aging of a whole generation of studio stars, epitomized in the aging faces of Bette Davis and Joan Crawford relegated to the genre of horror in *What Ever Happened to Baby Jane?* (1962), or the suicide of Marilyn Monroe. Crawford's face, perhaps more than any other screen star of the period, was a virtual battlefield of reterritorializations and deterritorializations. On-screen she mediated between the two limit-faces of Enlightenment being—between the despotic face of class and race privilege (and its sacrificial counterbodies) and the passional subjective face of contractual authority—the face of individuated bourgeois identity.

Crawford's signature performances embodied the bourgeois face of passional subjectivity in torsion, the faciality that Deleuze and Guattari describe as a "faciality of consciousness and passion, a redundancy of resonance and coupling" (184). In its bourgeois incarnation, this faciality overcodes representations of individuated identity subject to authoritarian order, contractual proceedings, and self-discipline (184). Rather than the expanding reterritorializations of the despotic regime of signs, which works through a "proliferation of black holes on the white wall," the passional subjective authoritarian face does not proliferate so much as resonate. This is the face of individuated identity, in the form of expression of "one hole cresting on an unravelling wall"—that is, in the form of expression of a continuity of subjectivized significations traversing a perpetually unfolding screen of destinal being (183–84). It proceeds by segmentary linearity, as in the endless segments of the melodramatic soap opera, rather than by radiating, proliferating circles, as in fashion's expansive exports of a repetitious sameness.[11]

If the despotic face and its sacrificial counterbodies reigned in noir detective mysteries, the passional subjective post-signifying face reigned in melodrama. Crawford's screen face was built on the fault lines between these two distinct semiotic systems—between the despotic and the authoritarian, between the white wall of proliferating significations and the black hole of consciousness and passion, and between their two distinct apparatuses of power—"despotic generalized slavery" and "authoritarian contract-proceeding" (181). That Crawford's face trembles between passional consciousness and despotic signification is symptomatic of a certain kind of (mal)function in feminine faciality in the post-World War II years. The madnesses that were perpetually seeping out of Crawford's face, or fleeing across it, were not aberrations but completely normative expressions of what Deleuze and Guattari identify as "the semiotic of capitalism"—a semiotic characterized by a "total interpenetration" of signification and subjectification (182). The public breakdowns signed in Crawford's screen face were nothing more than consumable representations of a common failure of "the sovereign organization of the face" to prevent the escape of deterritorialized faciality traits in the constant turbulences generated by the interpenetration of despotic and authoritarian facialities (188). In this regard, Crawford's face *was* the face of the Modern White Woman.

In *Mildred Pierce* (1945), Crawford becomes despotic, undergoing an incorporeal transformation from wife to divorcée and single mother, and then from waitress to wealthy proprietor on her way toward becoming the face of class privilege. On the level of visual signs, this transformation is carried out through fashionable changes in her wardrobe and expansive reterritorializations materialized in real estate. The conflict in the narrative is the conflict between the passional subjectivity of Mildred Pierce as working-class subject and her despotic faciality as wealthy property owner who attempts to buy the affection of her husband and daughter.

Whereas Crawford plays passional subjectivity becoming-despotic in *Mildred Pierce*, in *Humoresque* (1946) she plays the despotic face of the White Woman becoming the face of passional subjectivity on the way to the sacrifice. Crawford appears as the bearer of class privilege from the start of the film. As an independently wealthy married woman, she coldly takes a middle-class woman's boyfriend because she can further his career as a professional musician. Here, Crawford's face is the face of unveiled class privilege, greed, and excessive expenditure, but her face is also the face of alcoholism and, by the end of the film, suicide. *Humoresque* epitomizes the way in which the excesses of class and race privilege are embodied in the White Woman so that they can be contained on the level of representation by her scapegoating. In the process of this transformation, Crawford's face is produced as a consumable representation of bourgeois identity. On-screen, she gives the despotic signifier a human face even as she gives the human face of individuated bourgeois identity the power and seduction of class status. She can only do so, however, in the form of self-mutilation. After becoming the despotic faciality that legitimizes a decadent and excessive exercise of power and privilege, she begins a line of flight that ends in her own death, making her last call the call of passional self-sacrifice — in spite of the fact that from beginning to end her character consistently acts despotic, greedily snatching up and accumulating the objects, landscapes, and desires around her.

Crawford's alcoholic, suicidal flight in *Humoresque* is representative of the semiotic turbulence that both generated deviations in the White Woman's screen face and drew the limits of those deviations in the Hollywood cinema. Crawford's face was caught between the despotic face in decay and the face of passional subjective bourgeois identity in its moments of breakdown. If becoming-despotic was a nightmare, and defacializing despotism a slow trek toward suicide, becoming the passional subject of bourgeois authoritarian contract proceedings was equally

Passional subjective faciality caught in the nightmare of an authoritarian contract proceeding. Crawford presents the face of bourgeois subjective suffering during a scene in which her husband receives the shock treatment she has authorized. *Autumn Leaves*, directed by Robert Aldrich, 1956.

wrought with dangers and entrapments. In *Autumn Leaves* (1956), Crawford plays a spinsterly self-employed typist who marries a young disabled veteran suffering from posttraumatic stress as a result of war (screened in the film as an Oedipal trauma) who beats her and is incapable of holding a steady job. She resorts to the psychiatric institution, which prescribes electro-shock treatment and institutionalization — treatment she authorizes in an authoritarian contract proceeding turned into a melodramatic nightmare.

If authoritarian power legitimized by contract law was a flight from despotic faciality and its sacrifice, it nonetheless presented its own traps for feminine becomings. Contract proceeding and the abstract justice system that it authorized had its own mechanisms for facializing its subjects according to gendered biunivocalization. In spite of the reassurrances made in *Autumn Leaves*'s remarkable happy ending (the husband is miraculously "cured" and bears no resentment toward Crawford for his institutionalization), the film's audiences knew that contractual authority typically favored the masculinized and propertied subject. In addition, contract proceedings in theory may have protected women from sacrificial violence, but often enough they failed to do so in practice. And when they failed to do so, authoritarian contract proceedings merely worked as a screen for despotic sacrificial exchanges. Yet this faciality promised women the rights, privileges, and status of bourgeois individuated identity.

In David Lynch's *Blue Velvet*, Laura Dern plays the passional subjective face in the melodramatic subplot of a detective mystery gone awry. A surburban

Passional bourgeois subjectivity getting the call of betrayal,
domestic violence, and police corruption in the heart of the
heartland, U.S.A. Laura Dern in *Blue Velvet* (1986).

bourgeois version of a romantic heroine, she is caught in a postmodern melodrama/
horror film where her individuated subjectivity hits the limits of bourgeois agency.
She waits on the line within the nuclear cell of her suburban home for a call from
the couple-machine in the heart of the bourgeois heartland—the United States of
America. Instead, she gets the call of domestic violence and police corruption—interior breakdowns of the authoritarian hierarchy organizing oedipalized social relations. Lynch's representation of contemporary femininity in this regard is paradigmatically modern. The face of the feminine is split, like the film's narrative, between
despotic power and its sacrifice and passional bourgeois suffering, even as the feminine is produced as an amalgam of despotic and passional forms and substances of
expression.

The faciality organizing passional subjective identity has been a
major export from the United States to Latin American countries, where melodrama,
carried first through film and later broadcast via television, functioned as "a reflection of the North American capitalist system and as a principal producer of the capitalist subject (especially female ones)" (Lopez 597). Unlike the fashion system, which
overcoded class and race privilege, melodrama overcoded an "identification with
the gesture and expression of the actors," conveying a subjective referent for bourgeois identity appropriate for mass consumption via "emotional signification through
the closeup" (597, 603). Melodrama provided the marginalized a way to channel the
sacrificial signifier into a meaningful identity. It presented for mass consumption a
faciality of self-imposed restraint and introjected authority (and its constant breakdown) as a viable face of meaningful identity, one that made the social constraints
of being in the world bearable for the "underprivileged" or for the recipients of so-

cially condoned violences. Exported television melodrama presented passional being as a line of flight from despotic faciality and its sacrifice, even as it overcoded and extended the face of U.S. national identity onto Latin American markets.

Recently, this export industry and its flow of signs have been challenged by the emergence of the Hispanic "telenovela" as a major competitor with exported U.S. television programming in many Latin American countries, including Brazil, Venezuela, and Mexico. Telenovelas do differ from North American soap operas in several distinct ways; they have narrative closure, prime-time showings, and a broadcast audience that includes men and children as well as women (Lopez 600). But while telenovelas clearly deterritorialize exported U.S. television programming for the needs and desires of Latin American cultures, they continue to reproduce a major face of white capitalist society whenever they authorize a broadcast face of national or even transnational identity to stand in the place of unauthorized, local identities who bear the mark of difference. And while telenovelas are not exclusively marketed to women as television soaps are in the United States, they nonetheless overcode Latina and Latino identities as expressions of passional subjective authoritarian faciality through a process of biunivocalization, in which white gender codes map onto codes of race and class. Latino men, like Latina women and bourgeois white women, can see at least the reflection of their identities as individuated passional consciousnesses in the mirror of their suffering on broadcast television.

The popularity of the telenovela corresponds with the simultaneous solidification of and resistance against national and transnational capitalist political economies in Latin America. In this regard, the telenovela functions as part of a broadcast representational economy that works to appropriate indigenous populations bearing the marks of difference within the "unified" bourgeois identity of the nation-state. In the case of the Zapatista resistance in Chiapas, Mexico, in the mid-1990s, for example, organized local constituencies resisted being facialized as part of the Mexican national identity. Economically, these local constituencies provide a cheap labor force to harvest the rich natural resources of the Chiapas region and to transport those resources to the Mexican nation-state at large. But within this economy, local indigenous peoples can only be facialized within the "national" identity as invisible sacrificial bodies who live in poverty and whose labor is enslaved. Or, the more they resist national facialization, the more they can enter public mediation as the *visible* sacrificial signifier—"guerillas" who are enemies of the state and who must be put down by national armed forces. In this regard, the vast popularity of the telenovela may well represent a deterritorialization of the exported face of North American identity. But at the same time, the telenovela is an extension of the

A popular Hispanic soap imported to the United States displays
the passional face of local subjectivities in distress. The Latin
American telenovela is a deterritorialization—and
reterritorialization—of white mediated passional subjectivity.
From *Morena Clara*, produced by Venavision, Caracas, Venezuela;
distributed in the United States by Univision, Miami.

telemediated passional face of the capitalist subject into Latin American markets, and therefore a reterritorialization of differences within Latin American cultures into North American forms and substances of expression.

The faciality of passional subjective consciousness finds its limit in localized collective action—particularly if that collective action is resistant to nationalist identification. The face of the passional subject channels collective anger and outrage against past injustices toward individual suffering, individuated flights of passion, and sporadic individual action. Sign-flows generated by collective suffering, collective flights of passionate resistance or anger, spontaneous pack flows, or organized local action exceed the limit of this faciality machine. In other words, unauthorized organized action will exceed the limit of the passional signifying system if it cannot be translated into the isolated local action of an aberrative individual. Thus, media coverage of the Chiapas "uprising" focused on Zapatista leader "Subcommander Marcos" and his charismatic personality. In one communiqué responding to a report in the *San Francisco Chronicle* that Subcommander Marcos had once been fired from a restaurant for being gay, the Zapatistas released a statement to the press attempting to defacialize the face of the Zapatista movement as the individuated face of Marcos:

Marcos is gay in San Francisco, black in South Africa, an Asian in Europe, a Chicano in San Ysidro, an anarchist in Spain, a Palestinian in Israel, a Mayan Indian in the streets of San Cristobal, a gang member in Neza [a huge Mexico City slum], a rocker in the National

University [a folk music citadel], a Jew in Germany, an ombudsman in the Defense Ministry, a communist in the post-cold war era, an artist without gallery or portfolio.... A pacifist in Bosnia, a housewife alone on Saturday night in any neighborhood in any city in Mexico, a striker in the CTM, a reporter writing filler stories for the back pages, a single woman on the metro at 10pm, a peasant without land, an unemployed worker.... an unhappy student, a dissident amid free market economics, a writer without books or readers, and of course, a zapatista in the mountains of Southeast Mexico. So Marcos is a human being, any human being, in this world. Marcos is all the exploited, marginalized, and oppressed minorities, resisting and saying "Enough!" (Zapatista 1)

In bourgeois culture, if defacialized sign-flows cannot be contained within the limits of the individual, they may instantiate a threshold transformation in which the psychiatric institution and its categories of diagnosis appear as an apparatus of capture for deterritorialized becomings. Within the psychiatric regime of signs, the total breakdown of the faciality of the passional subjective individual may instantiate a diagnosis of psychosis, in which an unauthorized "redress seeker" is refacialized as the "monomaniac" (121). This process of semiotic translation *is* the instantiation of social power. As Deleuze and Guattari describe the process, when the "faciality machine translates formed contents of whatever kind into a single substance of expression, it already subjugates them to the exclusive form of signifying and subjective expression" (179). Translated into a form of psychosis and reduced to local sporadic acts, the monomaniac is typically a rural or underclass subject. In this, s/he differs from the bourgeois paranoid delusional produced in the breakdown of despotic faciality, who is caught up in the radiating circles of his or her own ideational delusions.

The difference between these two forms of psychosis is exemplified in the difference between the "monomaniac" Aileen Wuornos, a rural Florida street prostitute who murdered several of her johns and who was labeled by the media as a "serial killer" in the early 1990s, and Gloria Swanson playing the bourgeois delusional in the form of a faded Hollywood screen idol caught up in the radiating circles of her own self-absorbed significations in *Sunset Boulevard* (1950). In this regard, Deleuze and Guattari assert "a class based social order preserved even in delusion," with ideational bourgeois paranoiacs reproducing "a class with radiant irradiating ideas" and passional monomaniacs reproducing "a class reduced to sporadic local actions" (121).

By the 1960s, it was not just the screen idol's face that was degenerating into psychosis, but the Hollywood studio system itself as a concrete manifestation of an abstract expression-machine regulating the production of a consumable face of public femininity. Classic Hollywood during the studio years organized signification and subjectification according to a sensorimotor schema of individuated consciousness. Deleuze termed the vehicle of expression for this psychomechanics "the movement-image," of which the director Syberberg claimed the end product was Leni Riefenstahl's filmmaking under Hitler, and Benjamin the automatic movement that coincided with the automatization of the masses, and Krackauer the rise of the Hitlerian automaton (Deleuze 1989, 264). In this schema, the formal expression of continuity, anchored in the action-image, represented and reproduced the rational consciousness of bourgeois reality and social identities. The action-image assembled a continuity among the shot as unit of consciousness, the image as a unit of action and reaction, the narrative as a meaningful totality and causality of events in which events relate to the actions of individuals, the utterance as dialogue, and sound as a device for matching among all the components. This was the classic cinema's politics of representation and the mechanism by which it functioned as the sensorimotor organ of bourgeois individuated subjectivity. This organ would be deterritorialized and reterritorialized on several fronts during the decades after World War II.

The first challenge came from images from the war zone of World War II and its aftermath, conveyed to American audiences via Italian neorealist directors in the postwar years. The reality of the war was more fragmented and discontinuous than popular national narratives could explain. Popular films such as *Casablanca* (1942), starring Humphrey Bogart and Ingrid Bergman, and wartime propaganda films such as Frank Capra's *Why We Fight* series, had reassured American audiences that the "enemy" was "out there," in Germany, Italy, and Japan, leaving the public unprepared for the interior fascisms erupting from within the body politic at home. Violence leaked from the internal organs of U.S. nationalism in the postwar years, embodied in the 1953 sacrifice by electrocution of Ethel Rosenberg, a wife and mother, on charges of treason against the state during the worst years of McCarthyism.

But it was television and later video that facilitated the final collapse of the Hollywood studio system and its highly organized system of signs. As broadcast television became the privileged home of passional subjective faciality in its bourgeois forms, the classic cinema's highly organized system of signs was deterritorialized as it competed first with the televisual image, then with the video image, and later with the digitized image. The despotic face of white femininity was subject to degenerescence via excessive commodification of the feminine signifier in an economy of mechanical and later electronic reproduction and mass consumption. By the

The despotic signifier deterritorialized for private mass consumption. Porn face with tongue extended. *Penthouse Variations*, April 1995. Denied permission by *Penthouse*.

1960s, the classic cinema's once quality product was becoming a clichéd rerun commodity in a televisual economy of repetition. The feminine despotic signifier entered degenerescence as the face of Garbo was relegated finally to late-night movie channels, commercial breaks, and switchable programming. Eventually, the home video industry would further contribute to the decline of the despotic signifier's social value by placing the face of Garbo on a shelf of selections next to martial arts films, workout tapes, and soft and hardcore porn.[12]

Mass-produced pornography is the most obvious example of the effects of commodity logic on the public face of the feminine in a political economy of repetition and mass consumption. The economy of repetition that produced pornography as an $8-billion-a-year industry by 1984 demands both constant innovation and the speedy reproduction of formulaic products (Itzen). This systemic tension between innovation and repetition, between the new and the clichéd, shapes the form and substance of expression of the feminine. Porn, like fashion, works by exchanging an overcoded signifier for a desired social relation. For the vast majority of fashion consumers, fashion stands in the place of actual class privilege (you can buy fashion even if you don't have the property or accumulation of wealth that determines real class status, or, at the very least, you can buy the fashion magazine). Similarly, porn translates the desire for transgressive social relations into a purchase of the porn magazine (or video or web site). The pornographic transaction, as a completely legitimate business transaction, stands in the place of the actual transgression.

The difference between the fashionable face of femininity and the pornographic face is the difference between fashion's despotic regime of signs and porn as a deterritorialization of both the despotic signifier and authoritarian passional consciousness. Pornographic faciality recodes the despotic face of the White Woman as accessible to everyone regardless of class or race — that is, as available for mass consumption. At the same time, porn overcodes the simulacra of a withdrawal from the social in its dominant substance of expression — that is, linguistic exchange. In the pornographic face, this withdrawal from language and the social conventions conveyed and regulated through language is signified not in the eye but in the tongue.

Because grammatical relations are the ground of authoritarian contract proceedings, the exposed tongue of the erotic model functions as a "gesture of defiance of the grammatical order" and of the social contracts it legitimizes (MacCannell 164). In MacCannell's (1989) reading of the face in pornography, the extended tongue is a "double icon" representing both "erectile tissue in a state of sexual excitation" and "the antagonism between sex and language" (162–64). The extended tongue precludes articulate speech and invites a "sexually-based solidarity" (161, 173). This alternative solidarity is capable of overcoding everyday interactions and their usual grammatical categories, such as the categories of kinship, social status, race, age, and gender, by which discrete social bodies are organized and their exchanges regulated.[13]

Pornography turns a profit off the desire to flee authoritarian facialization, the desire to escape the grammatical relations that organize the social and that regulate appropriate(d) social identities. To the extent that this desire remains virtual, however, porn remains only the simulacrum of sexual solidarity, because it stands in the place of that solidarity, and because it channels the agency of the bourgeois subject back toward individuated forms of expression (i.e., toward masturbation and private consumption). Thus, while porn is the face of "antisocial" solidarity, "licentious withdrawal" from the social, and sexual defiance of the grammatical order, it is so only in a completely public, formulaic, mass-produced, and commodified form (172). In this regard, the face of pornography presents both a flight from authorized bourgeois identities and an apparatus of capture within an economy of "private" mass consumption.

The successful marketing of home video porn in the 1980s further devalued the cinematic screen woman's star status by overproducing a formulaic face of white femininity for inexpensive mass consumption with which the cinema would have to compete. On the cinema's state of crisis in an age of electronic media, Deleuze has commented, "If it is true that television kills cinema, cinema on the other hand is continually revitalizing television, not only because it feeds it with films, but because the great cinema authors invent the audio-visual image, which they are quite ready to 'give back' to television if it gives them the opportunity" (1989, 252). In the 1980s and 1990s, however, it was not just television but video and later digitized pornography that presented the latest challenge to the cinema and in part constituted the cinema in its postmodern substance of expression, for if it is true that porn kills the despotic face of the White Woman by devaluing her class and race privilege and making her accessible to everyone, the cinema also resurrects her so that it can give her back to erotica reassembled and revitalized. Disengaged from her sensorimotor organs, in a zone of rhizomatic flight, the public faciality of the White Woman has been both freed and forced to mutate, to disassemble and to reassemble, even as her flights have been captured between the two limit-faces of commercial pornography and informatics. These two limit-faces merge in interactive sex on TV—a merger which, while remaining as of yet virtual, is nonetheless on the electronic horizon.[14]

While mass-produced pornography sets one discursive limit for the public face of femininity, the electronic information industry sets another. Faced with the digital composition techniques of electronic multimedia so quickly assimilated and disseminated by advertising and MTV, the sensorimotor organ of bourgeois feminine identity suffered an irrational cut between sound and the visual image, between the grammatical order of the social and the syncretic flow of information and infotainment. The sensorimotor model based in the organic body, reproduced in continuity-style realism, and promulgated by the cinematographic image, was challenged not only by the televisual image (and its switchable programming) and the video image (and its economy of mass reproduction and home distribution), but also by the digital image (and its capabilities for hypermediation and hyperprocessing) and later the interactive image. It is not surprising in this context that such an economy of signs, based on repetition, multiple channels, and the constant flow of discontinuous signifying chains, would correspond socially with the breakdown of rational cognition in the form of schizophrenic disintegration or paranoid delusions. While the regime of signs constituting the subject in classic Hollywood correlated the automatization of movement with the automatization of the masses, the abstract-machine of informatics correlates the machinic "irrationality" of a syncretic sign-flow with psychopathology as a recognizable state of social being.

Whereas psychiatry projects an image of psychosis as an event or state occurring within the individual, the face of psychosis manifested in informatics occurs exterior to the individual, as a systemic breakdown of rational cognition within the general economy of signs. In psychoanalysis, psychosis is generally understood to be a foreclosure of the symbolic order resulting in states of delusion, "a disturbance of the libidinal relation to reality" (Laplanche and Pontalis 370). Inasmuch as the organic constitutes a ground zero of a material "real," a severe disturbance in the subjective relation to the organic, that is, a disturbance in the relation of the social face to the organic body, may well be the latest substance of expression of psychosis as a cultural (not individual) production (Morse 157).[15] The French multimedia performance artist Orlan has made a career of performing precisely this disturbance and recording or live-broadcasting the event as "art."

Combining digitized video with cosmetic surgery and baroque religious iconography, Orlan's early work did not represent but performed the disturbance between the organic body and the inorganic, socially reified, machinic face of the feminine, which she found as the core experience of plastic surgery. Using the face itself as her medium, cosmetic surgeons under her direction reconstructed her facial features to mimic classic artistic representations of women, changing her "chin into the chin of Botticelli's Venus (from *The Birth of Venus*), her nose into Psyche's nose (inspired by Gérard's *Le Premier Baiser de l'Amour à Psyché*), her lips to those of Europa in Moreau's *L'Enlèvement d'Europe*, her eyes to those of Diana in the painting of *Diane Chasseresse* by the School of Fontainebleau, and her forehead to resemble that of Leonardo da Vinci's *Mona Lisa*" (Popper 74).

Later, Orlan broke away entirely from these semiotic overcodings of feminine beauty, whether artistic or popular, entering a realm of signs beyond the biunivocalization of the beautiful and the ugly, perhaps even beyond the register of the human. In her latest "performance," a surgeon lifts the skin of her face from her forehead to her chin off its underlying tissue. On video projection, one strains to see what lies beneath this face of Orlan, beneath the fragile layer of skin. What one finds there is nothing more and nothing less than blood and tissue. Orlan's face, lifted from the skull, bleeds the abjection of the organic. When the surgery is done, she has had something looking like cheekbones constructed above her eyebrows. These structures show above her dark shades, which she often wears when addressing her audiences, while a large screen behind her reflects the projection of the production of the face in progress.

These performances display for public viewing the face of femininity not only as a production but as a symptom of the postmodern desire to assimilate the organic within the technological. Orlan's face is merely a reminder that all the technologically altered faces of femininity, from painting to plastic microsurgery, are symptoms of the common delusion that the organic can be appropriated as an artifact, subsumed within a technologized social, and projected as the object of an act of individual volition (Scarry 97). One can, after all, *choose* one's face, *can't one*? On this point, Orlan distinguishes her art — in which she chooses a face not based on socially accepted registers of beauty, femininity, or even humanity — from women who feel they must go to cosmetic surgeons in order to possess social standards of beauty or normality that they have incorporated.[16]

Indeed, choosing cosmetic surgery to alter facial/racial features to fit standards of normality is becoming a common practice among Asian American women in the San Francisco Bay area. Anthropologist Eugenia Kaw reported in 1993 that by 1988, 2 million Americans purchased cosmetic surgery, and that 87 percent of them were women. By 1988, the cosmetic surgery industry was grossing $300 million per year. By 1990, of all cosmetic surgery consumers, 20 percent were minorities, including Asian Americans (74). In the Bay area where Kaw produced her study, white women were commonly employing plastic surgery to enhance the breasts, remove body fat, and reduce wrinkles. Asian American women, in contrast, commonly employed plastic surgeons to refacialize Asian racial features in order to meet Western standards. The two most commonly requested procedures among Asian American women are eyelid reconstruction ("whereby folds of skin are excised from across their upper eyelids to create a crease above each eye that makes the eyes look wider") and nasal refinement ("surgical sculpting of the nose tip to create a more chiseled appearance, or the implantation of a silicone or cartilage bridge in the nose for a more prominent appearance") (75). These practices in cosmetic surgery only make manifest once again that the face is not organic. The body is organic, but the face is a social production, and as such it can be disintegrated from the organic body and reterritorialized as a more perfect expression of a socially constructed code.

The translation of the organic into the social often instantiates a delusional system, however, in that the organic stratum exceeds human volition, and cannot be entirely subsumed as a pliable artifact subject to the latest technologies of desire. The organic, bearing its own biochemical limits, returns as the return of the repressed within the contemporary political economy of signs in the substance and form of malignant neoplasties. In this regard, breast cancer is the organic ground zero of feminine faciality as a system of social significations mapped over the corporeal body. Cancer is what refuses to submit to the desires of a machinic social imaginary projected onto the technologized face of contemporary femininity. It is what remains beyond faciality, what returns to it as rupture, and what must be at all cost perpetually refacialized within intelligible limits of perception and signification. Breast cancer as a public sign, therefore, expresses first and foremost contamination: not only contamination from without, but contamination from within. The cancerous breast expresses not only a leak in technoculture's prosthetic maternal, seeping toxic productions into the landscape of modernity, but also cellular contamination from within, a malignant tumor that has burst through the smooth surface of the breast skin, rupturing feminine faciality as an intelligible and marketable surface of public signs.[17] Thus, to cover over this rupture symbolically, to screen the current breast cancer rate as a biological but not social pathology, to reconstruct artificial breasts in the place of loss, is to have engaged a delusional circuitry. Breast cancer is what in the organic contaminates the virtual face of femininity produced and marketed in the media. The face of breast cancer becomes a face of cultural psychosis when the social denies its own pathologies by projecting the malignant breast as pathology of the organic, and by covering over the site of the pathology with prostheses or reconstruction.

Even in state-authorized, public mediations of breast cancer *as* an epidemic, the structure of this delusional circuitry often emerges, to the extent that visual culture gives embodiment to a foreclosure of the symbolic over the organic — or a precession of a machinic imaginary over the organic body. The medical industry, for example, has invested heavily in imaging technologies that can identify and locate cancerous cell growth. This tendency reached a new height in 1992, when the United States Congress allocated $25 million in Department of Defense funding in the "fight" against breast cancer. Lisa Cartwright notes that the department spent the entire allocation on "optical and locational detection devices" (143). Cartwright points out the class, race, and cultural privilege structured into the distribution of such high-tech equipment, which typically does not find its way to municipal hospital systems where the death rate from breast cancer far exceeds the national average (145).

Furthermore, such photocentric focus on the tumorous growth *interior* to the individual body screens broader, social determinations of the breast cancer epidemic at large. As Cartwright puts it, "Many breast cancer activists are arguing this narrow focus on detection shortchanges research in such crucial areas as possible environmental and societal factors and genetic susceptibility" (144). In such an economy of representation, cancer always remains a pathology of the individuated body, not the social body, not the body politic. What can never be represented within this system of signs is the image of cancer as an expression of the social itself.

The relation between cancer rates and industrial carcinogens is a site of heated contention between the chemical industry and its researchers and experts in cancer prevention and advocacy groups for women's health.[18] One of the leading experts in cancer prevention, Samuel Epstein, reports, "Cancer now strikes one in three and kills one in four, up from an incidence of one in four and a mortality of one in five in the 1950s. Age-standardized incidence rates in the overall U.S. population have increased sharply by 43.5 percent from 1950 to 1988. Rates for some common cancers have increased more sharply: lung by 263 percent, prostate by 100 percent; and male colon and female breast by about 60 percent" (17).

In a press conference on February 4, 1992, in Washington, D.C., sixty-eight prominent U.S. experts in cancer prevention, carcinogenesis, epidemiology, and public health charged that the National Cancer Institute (NCI) had "minimized evidence for increasing cancer rates, which are largely attributed to smoking, trivializing the importance of occupational carcinogens as non-smoking attributable causes of lung and other cancers, and to diet per se, in spite of tenuous and inconsistent evidence and ignoring the important role of carcinogenic dietary contaminants" (Epstein 15). Asserting conflict of interest among members of the National Cancer Advisory Board and the Board of Overseers of the Sloan-Kettering Memorial Cancer Center, NCI's "prototype comprehensive cancer center," these experts in cancer prevention charged that many board members had interlocking financial interests with the cancer drug industry and with industries associated with environmental pollutants (20–23). With the exception of antismoking campaigns that assure us that cancer is attributable to an individual's behavior, only minimal funding was allotted to prevention of avoidable, industrial carcinogens in air, water, food, home, and the workplace (24). Experts in cancer prevention and public health also attacked NCI's "high fat" hypothesis of breast cancer as a "blame the victim" discourse that covered over preventable social causes of breast cancer such as carcinogenic pesticides and other dietary contaminants, not to mention the carcinogenic hazards of mammography itself (29–31).

Furthermore, NCI listed industrial pollution as being responsible for only 3 percent of cancer deaths in 1991, despite the fact that the manufacture of synthetic organic chemicals, particularly industrial carcinogens, increased from 1 billion pounds per annum in 1940 to 400 billion pounds annually by the 1980s (26, 31).

As for the relation between industrial and agricultural chemicals and breast cancer, six studies since 1976 have documented an increased risk for women's breast cancer associated with exposure to organochlorine pesticides and industrial chemicals such as dioxin, hexachlorobenzene, and polychlorinated biphenyls (PCBS) (Wasserman, Falk). Dioxin was produced in the manufacture of Agent Orange and is a common by-product of chemical processes for bleaching paper and tampons, among other things; hexachlorobenzene is used as an agricultural fungicide and wood preservative; PCBS, which are now banned in the United States, were used for several decades in electrical transformers, vacuum pumps, adhesives, fire retardants, hydraulic fluids, lubricants, and inks.[19]

In such a delusional economy, the cancerous breast becomes a rich market for the medical industry, which turns a tremendous profit by selling high-end images of the body's pathologies back to diseased consumers, along with treatment plans and reconstruction techniques based on the latest technologies. Those without health insurance, of course, do not have access either to these processes or to the latest technologies that determine them. Focused intently on the treatment of pathology, defined biologically, rather than on prevention, allopathic medicine helps to reproduce a delusional logic that denies the correspondences between the toxic productions of a machinic social and cancer rates.

By the early 1990s, the rate of breast cancer in the United States, according to the American Cancer Society, had reached one in nine (Brady).[20] Breast cancer is producing a new face of femininity—the mastectomy—which requires massive public mediation. At the same time, it is also producing a commercial market for cosmetic surgery that can ameliorate if not screen the banality of the cancerous breast in the American landscape. The mastectomized woman, to the degree that she signs the failure of the organic in technoculture, can yet be refacialized using the latest surgical technologies and techniques. In an economy that capitalizes on projecting inorganic surfaces over the organic body, refacializing breast cancer as a consumable face of femininity through postmastectomy reconstructive silicone-implant breast surgery is a "rational" enterprise—and a profitable industry. A feature article on surgical breast reconstruction in *Allure* magazine in 1995 demonstrates the media's role in popularizing radical methods of covering over the reality of breast cancer. The article featured a three-dimensional computer-generated image of a reconstructed torso using laser scans, suggesting that breast cancer could be, if not defeated by, at least remedied by, technology (Merrell).

My intention is not to criticize women who choose to have reconstruction, but rather to insist on the political importance of the public visibility

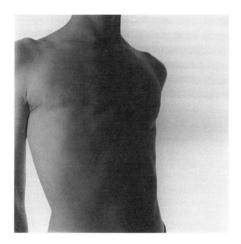

"Cancer is the most difficult, and the most meaningful,
experience of my life." Reclaiming the mastectomized body, from
the photo-essay "Cancer Destroys, Cancer Builds," by Stephanie
Byram, photographed by Charlee Brodsky. Copyright Brodsky
and Byram. Courtesy of Brodsky and Byram.

of breast cancer as a social epidemic.[21] To cover over the mastectomy scar in order
to provide individual women with a more normalized and therefore comfortable face
to live in is one thing. But to cover over the organic scar of technoculture's toxic
environment is another. It is this foreclosure of the symbolic in regard to breast
cancer as a social epidemic that makes the practice of reconstructive breast surgery
part of a face of cultural psychosis. To the extent that reconstructive breast surgery
serves not only a therapeutic function for the mastectomized woman but also a *signatory* function that helps to "normalize" this state of epidemic, it is the latest new
territory, the most recent symptom, and the last site of breakdown of the despotic
face of white femininity.

T W O

Lesbian Bodies in the Age of (Post)mechanical Reproduction

Becoming (Im)perceptible

Vanity Fair's August 1991 issue made a small splash amid the summer dust and heat following the Gulf War victory parades, arriving at many newsstands across the nation in a three-quarter-length brown paper wrapper sealed in plastic. The top of the magazine, which wasn't under cover, revealed *Vanity Fair*'s logo and Demi Moore's eyes looking directly and somewhat defiantly at the viewer. Beneath the brown wrapper, the discriminating consumer found Demi Moore sporting only a third-trimester pregnancy, a huge diamond earring, and an even huger diamond ring. On the cover, the pregnant and naked actress posed for a slightly angled profile shot down to the thigh, one arm cradling her pregnant belly, the other arm strategically covering her nipples. The caption read: "More Demi Moore." With the release of this issue, the fetishization of the maternal reached a new apex in the United States—it became 1990s fashion.

In the same month in the United States, early August 1991, the national lesbian and gay weekly *Gay Community News* featured a front-page photograph of a naked and very pregnant Susie Bright, known to lesbian communities, before her departure from the San Francisco lesbian sex magazine *On Our Backs*, as Susie Sexpert. Bright, like Moore, is posing for a slightly off-center frontal shot down to her thigh. One arm cradles her pregnant belly, while her hand makes a masturbatory gesture near her crotch. The other hand is placed strategically between her breasts so as to expose her nipples. She gazes invitingly at the viewer, smiling wryly in a man's top hat, vintage glasses, a leather harness handcuffed around the narrowest spot on her maternal torso (just below the breastline), and a leather-thong garter around one thigh. One can make out a trace of nonairbrushed pubic hair beneath her unmanicured hand. The headline read: "Photographic Examinations of the DEMI MONDE."

The synchronicity of, yet disjunctions between, these two popular images of women is the crucial signifier in this intertext about feminine identities in postmodern culture.[1] Bright's photograph, with the newspaper's headline, is a direct mimicry of *Vanity Fair*'s "straight," but itself unusual, cover issue — an issue that successfully, and for the first time, assimilated both the maternal *and* the nude into mainstream fashion photography.

Certainly, lesbian bodies pursue lines of flight from dominant biunivocal constructions of the feminine and masculine, in which the woman functions as lynchpin to a heterosexual sex-gender system of exchange. Contemporary lesbian bodies, however, are disorganized bodies of signs occupying a reterritorialized space of capitalism in which the notion of "woman" is being substantively and materially rewritten — but with no guaranteed outcomes and no promise of transcendent finality. The situation of contemporary lesbian social bodies makes intelligible from yet another point of view that the notion of the original is both a seduction and a ruse.

The Demi Moore/Susie Bright juxtaposition serves to remind us that both these differential flows of becoming-woman participate in the repetition of popular clichés organizing the disorganized bodies of the feminine into recognizable social identities. The repetition and variance between the *Vanity Fair* and *Gay Community News* covers provide a figure for two differential yet simultaneous flows of contemporary femininities. Aided by Bright's popular insistence that she be read as a lesbian body of signs, I begin this mapping of lesbian bodies both within and without "femininity," in popular sites where lesbians are more visible, before moving to cultural sites where the mainstreaming of lesbian bodies of signs is both more encrypted within and more appropriative of straight regimes of signification, and therefore more subject to shared reading protocols for identification of lesbian signification. It's perfectly telling that pursuing the visible lesbian body leads directly to the sex industry.

Bright's visibility as a self-determined pop-cultural icon of lesbianism and as a spokesperson for lesbian sexualities and sex-positive lesbian feminism makes it easier to register the relation of a "minority" social identity articulated as a *collective* social identity to the cultural repertoire of dominant clichés of the feminine. Functionally, *Vanity Fair*'s August cover was meant to signify the magazine's difference (at least for the month of August) from other society journals, fulfilling the perpetual performativity criterion of commodity logic in an economy of repetition. But the cover also signified a historical difference from past images of women. Both orders of difference signify by playing off a number of clichés: fashion's cover girl, the gentleman's centerfold, the cultural figure of the prima donna, and the artistic figure of the madonna. The crucial distinction of the *Vanity Fair* cover is its assemblage of repetitive clichés in one issue. The pregnant madonna—an image that stands out vividly against a long artistic history of postpartum madonnas— is at the same time the fashion statement and the sexualized object of the viewer's gaze.[2] And this viewer can no longer be delimited as only male.

The *Gay Community News*'s parodic re-presentation of the Demi Moore cover depends, in its turn, on the *Vanity Fair* parody in order to signify itself as difference. Bright's body of signs is a loaded contrast to Demi Moore's straight image. Rather than bear the signs of social status and fashion (Moore's diamond jewelry and the airbrushed aestheticization of her body image), Bright bears the signs of queer sexual identity and its ritualized deterritorializations of social status and power relations (S/M leather bondage toys, crossdressing, and an aberrant autoeroticism). Her not airbrushed image challenges not only traditional tropes of heterosexual femininity in the mass media, but also common stereotypes of lesbians as nonmaternal, masculinized women with "PC" consciousness who abhor pornography, hate men, and never really have sex (certainly not penetration).[3] The *Gay Community News*'s front page allows sexual mothers, pregnant lesbians, and identifying readers to signify simultaneously as difference and sameness.

In the case of the two popular media images of Moore and Bright, it becomes absurd to ask which of these is the "real" woman. To further complicate the assumption of an "original" in this case of reproduction, we have to note that Bright's image—an apparent parody of Demi Moore's—actually preceded *Vanity Fair*'s August 1991 issue by more than a year. The photo recontextualized by *Gay Community News* was taken from Michael Rosen's *Sexual Portraits*, published in 1990. Bright's daughter was born in the summer of that year. In this regard, the Demi Moore cover photograph was already a straight appropriation of a lesbian body of signs. The obscurity of origins in this case points again to the role cultural clichés play in the reproduction of signs and identities in an economy of repetition. In Michael Rosen's sexual portrait, Bright makes up the difference of her identity from the material signs at hand (motherhood, sex toys, man's hat, etc.), that is, from the cultural

Susie Bright posing as transgendered madonna in *Sexual Portraits:
Photographs of Radical Sexuality* (Shaynew
Press, 1990). Photo copyright Michael Rosen.
Courtesy of Michael Rosen.

repertoire of gendered codes. Obviously, Bright didn't parody Moore in particular when she positioned her body for Rosen's portrait; she parodied a cultural condition of femininity in general.

The cultural context of Bright's deterritorializations of gender and her marketing of her self-image as postmodern genderfuck clearly arises from the San Francisco sex industry of the 1980s and 1990s. Her flamboyant (i.e., queer-camp) style of parodic mimicry and wry humor in her writings on lesbian sex and eroticism have made her, along with Pat Califia, one of the most successful writers to popularize sex-positive lesbianism in the United States.[4] What Cindy Sherman's parodic self-portraits have helped to make intelligible for the museum and art-photography crowd, Bright's column ("Toys for Us" in *On Our Backs*, 1984 to 1990), traveling lectures ("How to Read a Dirty Movie," "All Girl Action," and safe-sex demos), books (*Susie Sexpert's Lesbian Sex World* [1990] and *Susie Bright's Sexual Reality: A Virtual Sex World Reader* [1992]), and guest appearances (as a "bisexual" on *The Donahue Show* in 1991 and as a dildo salesgirl in Monika Treut's 1988 film *Virgin Machine*) have helped make visible to popular audiences, both straight and queer, that being in the feminine and *out* entails deterritorializations of the text of identity as it is written across the body itself.

In this regard, Bright's popularized lesbian body of signs exemplifies the double bind of contemporary collective social identities grounded in sexual practices and sexual identities. The sexual line of flight by which Bright's popularized, sex-positive lesbianism marks its social identity *as* difference is reterritorialized by the commercial sex industry. The popular lesbian is most "out" and visible in contemporary U.S. culture, where the terrain of sexuality is regulated and appropriated by the sex industry's commercialization of "lesbian" sex. In this cultural terrain, sex-positive lesbians flee the law of heterosexual exchange by overtly investing in the workings of commodity logic in an attempt to win in the exchange more public visibility. The result is that the lesbian can appear in public in the delicate space between the two limit-faces of commercial pornography and obscenity. Precisely because it pursues a sexual line of flight from heterosexual reproduction and exchange while exchanging commodified sexual practices for social visibility, the sex-positive lesbian feminist movement runs a far greater risk than the straight women's movements of evoking the gaze of a popular fascist imaginary at a time of family values coalitions and a highly mediated new right actively projecting a paranoid discourse of decadence onto queer bodies and signs. The lesbian can appear as porn at the same time that she must be censored as the obscene.

At the heart of decadent discourse lies the idea of an organic social totality—the harmonious integration of parts toward a unified whole—as the legitimation criterion for a "healthy" social body. "Decadence" implies the degenerescence of such an organic social totality. Self-proclaimed decadent movements are often represented by dominant society as cults of sickness and decay, and historically are often purged as such by antidecadent movements, as they were in Germany during the rise of fascism in the 1930s. From the point of view of so many "decadent" artists and writers, however, they are simply representing the sicknesses already existing in the so-called "healthy" social body—a body that, by definition, would have to contain each occurrence of decay as external to itself. It is not surprising, then, that the history of decadent movements is also the history of the scapegoating of nonnormative (i.e., "deviant") social bodies as pariahs.

While Bright's public image of lesbianism was going mainstream, other representations of lesbians were under attack by overt censorship. One of these representations was a collection of lesbian photographs by "supreme out dyke and art photographer" Della Grace published in Britain by GMP in 1991. When her book

Love Bites was shipped from Britain to the United States, U.S. Customs seized all copies of the book and requested permission to destroy them from the U.S. distributor, Alyson Books. Alyson threatened court action, and in the end Customs let the books through.

It would be easy to think that the five-page section of the book titled "Ruff Sex" was what evoked the charge of obscenity. Certainly this graphic photographic representation of a ménage à trois featuring penetration with a dildo in what looks like the back room of a bar is not your usual public portrayal of femininity. Was here, finally, a realistic representation of sex between women that qualified as "hard core"? In actuality, however, there was something far more insidious about the book—there was a general and pervasive perversity about the photographs that evoked the threat of censure. That perversity was the book's deviant deterritorializations of the normative categories of class, race, and gender. Grace had imaged biracial couples, phallic women with dildos, a wedding ceremony between two leather dykes, gay pride and protest marchers, and the variegated tribes of the underground lesbian bar scenes in London and San Francisco from 1983 to 1990. What was obscene about *Love Bites* was that it represented phallic (rather than maternal) lesbian bodies as a community rather than an object for consumption. These photographs were not designed to go mainstream. More than images of consumption, they seemed intended to move the subjects of Grace's gaze toward a communal identity via the public eye of art photography.

Love Bites is in effect a history book as much as an art book, documenting nearly a decade of urban lesbian subculture in images that provide an identificatory location for the subjects being gazed upon as well as for those who gaze. Single women and couples are each given first names, signifying their status in the "real" while slipping the legacy of the patronym: Jess, Ruth, Issy and Beccy, Jane, Jane, Queen of Pain, Leslie and Billy, Lois and Eve, Kitchoo and Sarah, Robyn and Angie. Places in lesbian subculture are named: The Bell, Zombies, Pussies Galore, Club Uranus, Venus Rising, Cafe San Marcos, Chain Reaction, Scott's Bar. Acts are named: "harnessed," "permission to play," "be my bitch," "the ceremony," "love bites." And events are given names: San Francisco Gay Freedom Day 1990; Stop the Clause March, London 1988; Lesbian Strength March, London 1988; Lesbian and Gay Pride March, London 1988. And throughout the text, the social and sexual practices by which these lesbians can identify themselves as a community and as a historical social presence are given visual record.

Love Bites literally embodies a collective social identity not only by putting forth its bodies for a public gaze but also by publicly gazing at its own

San Francisco Gay Freedom Day. Dykes on Bikes.
From *Love Bites*. Courtesy of Della Grace.

collective social body — and thereby translating a disorganized body of signs into a collective lesbian community — *an organized social body* — that crosses national, class, and racial borders. While *Love Bites* exposed the limits constraining the sex-positive lesbians' entry into mainstream culture as an *already existing* deviant subculture, other signs of lesbian identities proliferated and were being quickly assimilated in the mediated public sphere. It was becoming increasingly unclear in popular culture exactly what constituted a "lesbian" signifier.

Becoming-Majoritarian

What signs mark the presence of a lesbian body?

Writing the lesbian body has become more common of late, making reading it all the more difficult. Less hidden, and so more cryptic than ever, the lesbian body increasingly appears as an actual variability set within the decors of everyday discourses. Signs of her presence appear on the cover of *Elle*, for example, or in popular film and paperback detective mysteries as both the sleuth *and* femme fatale, in texts that range from Mary Wing's overt lesbian thriller *She Came Too Late* (1987) to the conflicted, symptomatic lesbian subplot in Bob Rafelson's *Black Widow* (1986). She appears disguised as a vampire in Tony Scott's *The Hunger* (1983), and masquerading as the latest American outlaw hero in *Thelma and Louise* (1991). On television, she's making her appearance on the evening soap *L.A. Law*, and she virtually made MTV via Madonna's *Justify Your Love* music video (1990). When MTV censored the video, she appeared on ABC's *Nightline* instead, under the guise of "news." Elsewhere, in the latest lesbian mail-order video from Femme Fatale — a discursive site where the lesbian imaginary meets the sex industry — you can find her on all fours and dressed in leather or feathers, or leather *and* feathers, typically wearing a phallic silicone simulacrum. Amid controversy, she appeared in the trappings of lesbian bar culture in San Francisco and London passing as a collection of art photographs in Della Grace's *Love Bites* (1991). In the summer of 1992, PBS broadcast a BBC production depicting the torrid affair between Violet Treyfusis and Vita Sackville-West into the living rooms of millions of devoted viewers as part of Masterpiece Theatre, with an introduction by Alistair Cook. Meanwhile, Susie Bright made more lesbian sexual reality in 1992 with her new *Susie Bright's Sexual Reality: A Virtual Sex World Reader*, published by Cleis Press and quickly selling out of its first printing. Lesbian computer nerds quietly wait for Bright to assist in the world's first virtual sex program designed by a lesbian. Same-sex sex between women is already a menu option on the popular on-line *Virtual Valerie*, along with a menu for a variety of sex-toy applications. Let's face it: lesbian bodies in postmodernity are going broadcast, they're going technoculture, and they're going mainstream.[5]

In the process of mainstreaming, in which minoritarian and majoritarian significations intermingle, the lesbian body of signs is exposed as an essentially dis-organ-ized body.[6] *The* lesbian is as fantasmatic a construct as *the* woman. There are women, and there are lesbian bodies—each body crossed by multiplicitous signifying regimes and by different histories, different technologies of representation and reproduction, and different social experiences of being lesbian determined by ethnicity, class, gender identity, and sexual practices. In other words, as lesbian bodies become more visible in mainstream culture, the differences among these bodies also become more apparent. There is a freedom and a loss inscribed in this current cultural state of being lesbian. On one hand, lesbians are given greater exemption from a categorical call that delimits them from the cultural spaces of the *anytime, anywhere*. On the other hand, the call of identity politics becomes increasingly problematic.

The problem of identity is always a problem of signification in regard to historically specific social relations. Various attempts have been made to locate a lesbian identity, most inculcated in the grand nominalizing imperative bequeathed us by the Victorian taxonomies of "sexual" science. Should we define the lesbian by a specific sexual practice, or by the lack thereof? By a history of actual, or virtual, relations? Can she be identified once and for all by the presence of a public, broadcast kiss, by an act of self-proclamation, or by an act of community outing? Should we know her by the absence of the penis, or by the presence of a silicone simulacrum? Surely this material delimitation may go too far—for shouldn't we wonder whether or not a lesbian text, for all that, can be written across the body of a "man"? I can point to the case of male-to-female transsexuals who cathect toward

Club Uranus, San Francisco. From *Love Bites.*
Courtesy of Della Grace.

women, but why should we limit the problematic to its most obvious, symptomatic manifestation?[7]

The question of a lesbian body of signs always takes us back to the notion of identity in the body, of body as identity, a notion complicated in postmodernity by alterations in technologies of reproduction. Benjamin observed in "The Work of Art in the Age of Mechanical Reproduction" (1978), written on the eve of World War II, that symptomatic alterations in technologies of reproduction would have significance far beyond the realm of art (221). In fact, alterations in the status of the work of art as a historical object, which Benjamin maintained was analogous to the "natural" object, were already caught up during the rise of German fascism with alterations in the status of the subject and the subject's "collective" identity in relation to an increasingly destabilized notion of "nature" as original presence. Benjamin wrote unaware of the final atrocities that were to be carried out in the name of cleansing both the cultural heritage of the German state and those social bodies who would embody that heritage. Yet, already he could see the irony of the fascist mode of operation: while launching an ideological campaign for traditional cultural values, fascist organizations embraced all forms of machinic reproduction, even though the plurality of copies produced by mechanical reproduction produced the very devaluation of "original" objects (and subjects) that signified the liquidation of the traditional value of the cultural heritage.

Forgoing any of the nostalgias for traditional cultural heritages that mobilized fascist discourses of cultural decadence and degenerescence, of purity and cultural cleansing, I map contemporary lesbian bodies in this chapter as subjects of history who have entered a number of becomings, both as a resistance to and an outcome of the cultural logic and political economy of later capitalism. Applying

Deleuze and Guattari's nonarborescent method in *A Thousand Plateaus*, I premise here that contemporary forms of expression of lesbian bodies are produced by rhizomatic, not oppositional, relations to a multiplicity of majoritarian and minoritarian others—including but not limited to straight femininity, straight feminism, straight masculinity, and gay masculinity.[8]

Certainly, lesbians embody lines of flight from biunivocal constructions of the feminine and the masculine, in which "the woman" functions as lynchpin to a heterosexual sex-gender system of exchange. Contemporary lesbian bodies, however, are disorganized bodies of transformation, occupying a deterritorialized space of capitalism in which the notion of "woman" is being substantively and materially rewritten—but with no guaranteed outcomes and no promise of transcendent finality. The situation of contemporary lesbian social bodies illustrates that the notion of the "original" in the domain of identity is both a seduction and a ruse obscuring existing investments in the cultural logic of postmodernity.

Benjamin also observed in his analysis of the political economy of mechanical reproduction that mechanical reproduction destroyed the aura of the original work of art and, more importantly, provided a circuit for mass mentalities and thus an access code for fascism in the twentieth century.[9] We might recall in regard to this observation Hitler's admission that without the electronic reproduction of his voice over the radio, he could never have conquered Germany. For the sake of thinking about the future of lesbian bodies in postmodernity, I want to recall Benjamin's critique of the state's techno-fetishization of technologies of reproduction in the context of contemporary lesbian bodies—bodies working under a signifying regime of simulation and within an economy of repetition. Baudrillard (1983) has defined postmechanical reproduction as the precession of simulacra, the accession of post–World War II, postindustrial culture to a state of hyperreality. This state is reached when cultural reproduction begins to refer first and foremost to the fact that there is no original. For Attali (1985), postmechanical reproduction marks the difference between an economy of representation, in which representative power is used to maintain belief in the harmony of the socius, and an economy of repetition, characterized by the repetitive mass production of all social relations and the silencing of disorder by a bureaucratic power that operates in the ambience of a deafening syncretic flow. The cultural reproduction of lesbian bodies in the age of (post)mechanical reproduction, that is, in an economy of simulacral repetition, has more than ever destroyed any aura of an "original" lesbian identity, while exposing the cultural sites through which lesbianism is appropriated by the political economy of postmodernity.

Benjamin noted that the aesthetic debates over the status of photography as "art" obscured the more crucial question of whether the invention of photography hadn't transformed the very nature of art. Similarly, the appearance of the public lesbian, particularly after World War II liberated her from a depression economics, raises the question of whether the "nature" of the feminine hasn't substantively changed in postmodern culture. The point is that the political economy of (post)mechanical reproduction is altering traditional values and expressions of gendered social identities as subjects of history.

The subjective transformation that Benjamin was on the verge of articulating in the years approaching World War II involved the relation of technologies of representation to the human body in regard to identification. In Benjamin's reading of the broader effects of photography and film, the audience's identification had shifted from the actor (Hitler) to the camera (technology). Technical reproduction not only changes the reaction of the masses to art, it calls the masses into being in their late-modern and postmodern forms as subjects, not of nature, but of technology.[10]

We are at a moment of culture, for example, when phallic body prostheses are being mass-produced in the merger of the sex industry with plastics technologies. *On Our Backs* is not the only photojournal to market artificial penises. Even *Playgirl*, marketed primarily to straight women, carries pages of advertisements for a huge assortment of phallic simulacra. We're left to wonder what these women might eventually think to do with a double-ended dildo. But there's no mistaking that the lesbian assimilation of the sex-toy industry is reterritorializing the culturally constructed aura of the phallic signifier. By appropriating the phallus/penis for themselves, lesbians have turned technoculture's semiotic regime of simulation and the political economy of consumer culture back against the naturalization of masculinist hegemony. Once the penis is mass-reproduced, any illusion of a natural link between the cultural power organized under the sign of the phallus and the penis as biological organ is exposed as artificial. The reproduction of the penis as dildo exposes the male organ as signifier of the phallus, and not vice versa; that is, the dildo exposes the cultural organ of the phallus as a simulacrum. The dildo is an artificial penis, an appropriated phallus, and a material signifier of the imaginary ground for a historically manifest phallic regime of power.

The effect on lesbian identities of this merger between the sex industry and plastics technologies is typical of the double binds characteristic of lesbianism in postmodernity. Ironically, the validity of grounding phallic power and gendered identity in the biological sign of difference in the male body is set up for cultural reinvestigation and reinvestment once the penis itself is reproduced as signifier, that is, in the very process of mass-producing artificial penises as a marketable sign for the consumption of desiring subjects, including subjects desiring counterhegemonic identities. At the same time, the commodification of the signifier—in this case the penis as signifier of the phallus—obscures the politico-economic reproduction of straight class relations by channeling lesbian signification from the unstable and uncertain register of the *Real* to the overly stable, imaginary register of desire of the fetish-sign (i.e., the repetitive channeling of desire into the fixed circuit that runs from the penis as phallus to the phallus as penis in an endless loop). In other words, if working-class and middle-class urban lesbians and suburban dykes cannot afford health care and do not yet have real national political representation, they can nonetheless buy a ten-inch "dinger" and a matching leather harness, and they can, with no guarantees, busy themselves at the task of appropriating for lesbian identities the signs of masculine power. This situation provides *both* a possibility for self-reinvention and self-empowerment *and* an appropriation of lesbian identities—and their labor, their leisure, and their purchasing power—into the commodity logic of technoculture.

At the same time, new reproductive technologies, including artificial insemination by donor (AID), in vitro fertilization (IVF), surrogate motherhood, Lavage embryo transfer, and tissue farming (as in cross-uterine egg transplants), are both reterritorializing and reifying biological relations to gendered social roles (Corea 1986, Overall 1989). The "body" is breaking up. I'm not talking just about the working body, the confessing body, the sexual body. These are old tropes, as Foucault (1980) showed us. In postmodernity, even the organs are separating from the body. That these organs are literal makes them no less organs of power. The womb is disjunct from the breast, for example, the vagina from the mouth that speaks, the ovaries and their production from the womb, and so on. The lesbian body's relation to these reified technologies is entirely representative of the contradictions of lesbian subject positions in postmodernity. While new reproductive technologies generally reinforce a repressive straight economy of maternal production, body management, and class-privileged division of labor, the technology of cross-uterine egg transplants, though highly regulated economically, finally allows a lesbian to give birth to another lesbian's child, a fact that to date has gone entirely unmentioned by both the medical community and the media.[11]

The point is that the bodies that are the supposed ground of identity in essentialist arguments—arguments that assert we are who we are because of our bodies—are both internally fragmented in response to the intrusions of bio-technologies and advanced surgical techniques, including transsexual procedures, and externally plied by a variety of technologically determined semiotic registers ranging from the sex-toy industry to broadcast representation. As a result, lesbian identities are generating a familiar unfamiliarity of terms, which San Francisco's lesbian sexpert, Susie Bright, has busily been mainstreaming on *The Phil Donahue Show*—terms as provocative as *female penetration*, *female masculinity*, *S/M lipstick dykes*, and *lesbian phallic mothers*.

While all social bodies are plied by multiple regimes of signs, as Deleuze and Guattari as well as Foucault have repeatedly shown, lesbian bodies in the age of (post)mechanical reproduction are particularly paradigmatic of a radical semiotic multiplicity. This situation is hardly surprising. That lesbians are *not* women because women are a class defined by their relation to men—a statement Monique Wittig (1992) has popularized—doesn't mean we know exactly what a lesbian is. The "lesbian," especially the lesbian who resists or slips the always potential sedimentarity in that term, marks a default of identity both twice removed and exponentially factored. Lesbians in the public culture of postmodernity are subjects-in-the-making whose body of signs and bodies as sign are up for reappropriation and revision, answering as they do the party line of technology and identity.

This double call of technology and identity complicates our understanding of lesbian bodies as minority bodies—a definition that locates lesbians within the discourse of identity by their differences from the majority bodies of the hetero woman and man. If Wittig (1992) wants to envision lesbians as "runaway slaves with no other side of the Mississippi in sight," perpetual and permanent fugitives, it's also undeniable that lesbians are at the same time, and often in the same bodies, lesbians bearing arms, lesbians bearing children, lesbians becoming fashion, becoming commodity subjects, becoming Hollywood, becoming the sex industry, or becoming cyborg human-machinic assemblages. And from the alternative point of view, we are also bearing witness to the military becoming lesbian, the mother becoming lesbian, straight women becoming lesbian, fashion and Hollywood and the sex industry becoming lesbian, middle-class women, corporate America, and technoculture becoming lesbian. That is, the lesbian body of signs, like all minority bodies, is always becoming majority, in a multiplicity of ways. But at the same time, in a multitude of domains across the general cultural field, majority bodies are busy *becoming lesbian*.[12] This notion of the transsemiotics of identities follows from Deleuze and Guattari's schizoanalysis of the postulates of linguistics, in which the linguistic notion of minority language produces its meaningful variance from a rhizomatic, not oppositional, relation to its majority others.

In the lesbian cultural landscape of postmodernity, essentialist arguments about feminine identity are more defunct than ever, while Wittig's lesbian materialist analysis of straight culture is more urgent than ever and more problematic. Even if the first social contract underpinning dominant class relations in later industrial capitalism is still the heterosexual contract, as Wittig premises in *The Straight Mind*, the cultural variables for negotiating the space of that social contract are undergoing reconfiguration in postmodernity in ways that Wittig overlooks. This is why it's crucial to think the question of contemporary lesbian bodies in the specific context of the breakdown of ontological discourses in the shift from modernity to postmodernity, because in that shift the Cartesian, total subject that Wittig wants to claim as a right and as the political goal of lesbian identity politics is more and more manifestly undergoing splittings and fragmentations.[13] The decentralization of the post-Cartesian subject of postmodern culture is not antithetical to the dis-organ-ized political economy of postindustrial society, as Deleuze and Guattari have argued in the two volumes of *Capitalism and Schizophrenia* (1983, 1987). Indeed, capitalism itself produces schizoid subjectivity as a cultural state of being. For example, the notion of self in consumer discourse as a state that can be perpetually reconstructed according to one's desire, and the reification of that desire into the reproduction of class relations has, in the case of lesbians, set a political economy of signs based on the commodification of selves in contention with compulsory heterosexuality and the cultural function it and the nuclear family serve in reproducing the labor force.

Setting lesbian identities first within the context of postmodern culture suggests two further clarifications to Wittig. First, any materialist analysis of a lesbian revolutionary position in relation to straight women as a class has to begin with one irreducible conundrum of postmodernity in regard to lesbian identities. The cultural space for contemporary lesbian identities to exist—economic freedom from dependence on a man—was a historical outcome of late industrial capitalism's commodity logic in its total war phase in the first half of the twentieth century.[14]

Most historians of the gay and lesbian movement in American culture recognize the role played by the military-industrial-labor complex in creating the conditions in which such a movement could emerge. Demographic shifts toward urban centers during the prewar and wartime years set the stage for a transformation in the relation of the homosexual "secret" to the public sphere. As D'Emilio describes the process,

The relocation of civilians of both sexes to the burgeoning centers of defense industry typically involved a shift from rural and small-town residences to impersonal metropolitan areas. Young adults who in peacetime might have moved directly from their parents' home into one with their spouse experienced instead years of living away from kin and away from settings where easygoing intimacy with the opposite sex led to permanent ties. Families endured prolonged separation, divorce and desertion occurred more frequently, and the trend toward greater sexual permissiveness accelerated. (23)

If the military's organizational needs and transportation networks during mobilization for total war brought gays and lesbians together in huge demographic centers, the military's postwar purges of gays and lesbians during the McCarthy years helped to fortify gay and lesbian solidarity in the major port cities, where queer enlisted personnel were often discharged. D'Emilio notes that at the end of the 1940s, homosexual "separations" from the military averaged around 1,000 per year; by the early 1950s, the rate of discharges had doubled, and that figure had doubled again by the early 1960s (44). Women serving in the Women's Army Corps (WAC) and Women Accepted for Voluntary Emergency Service (WAVES) were not exempt from either the military's substitute bodies recruitment policies during total war or its postwar purging practices.

Women, particularly single women, made up a large proportion of the substitute bodies required by the state to maintain the performativity criteria and accelerated industrial needs of total war and reconstruction. This is one of the undeniable conditions of women's entry into the workforce and the professions in the United States, including the academy, and of their assimilation into the commodity marketplace beyond the domestic sphere, which, along with the 1960s civil rights movement, helped to set up the possibility of the 1970s women's movement.[15] This is also part of the history of the cultural production of lesbian bodies as we know them today.

In other words, and this is my final clarification to Wittig's reading of lesbian positionality, lesbians are becoming nomad runaways *and* becoming state *at the same time*. And it's at the various sites where these interminglings of bodies take place that the cultural contradictions will be most apparent and therefore the political stakes greatest. These sites include any becoming majoritarian of the minoritarian as well as the becoming minor of majority regimes of signs, and in each of these sites the political stakes may not be equivalent. This political complication results from the theoretical challenge to materialist social analysis presented by the failure of poststructural linguistics to adequately map cultural dialects *except* as unstable and constant sites of transformation. These kinds of subcultural variance and continuous historical transformation have to be factored into any lesbian materialist modeling system if we are to continue the work Wittig has launched not only toward a lesbian materialist critique of straight-class relations, but toward a materialist critique of lesbianism itself.

A discursive multiplicity of differences has to be seen as *both* a pragmatics of appropriation by straight culture and as signs of actual historical and material differences within subcultural groups. It's not enough to say that our discursive differences obfuscate the material reproduction of our class relations. Yet the material manifestations of the discourse of technology have made the lines between discourse, culture, and actual social bodies increasingly difficult to distinguish. If Wittig would identify lesbians by their refusal to take on the identity of the class that provides the labor and bodies for reproducing the labor force, for example, that distinction can no longer be so easily made. Reproductive technologies and economic independence have made it even more common for lesbian bodies to be maternal bodies, if not maternal bodies bearing the phallus. The materialist mapping of lesbian identities in postmodernity will therefore have to calculate relations among commodity logic, racially segmented and gendered classes, technologies of reproduction and simulation, and a war-machine partially exterior to the state in spite of its historical appropriation under the regime of global security and within the military-industrial-labor-foreign aid complex. Consider, for example, the yet hypothetical but virtually real instance of the feminine cyborg assemblage made manifest in a female F-16 pilot executing desert bombing raids. When this virtual state of events becomes actual, my first question will be, "Is she a lesbian body?"

Cultural mappings of lesbian bodies will also have to include interminglings among "minorities." These specific sites of mixing and transformation will shape the political stakes and the political strategies for a lesbian-feminist-queer nation alliance, and any possible alliance between that configuration and ethnic minorities. Take the case, from the 1950s to the present, of lesbians becoming only with much difficulty lesbian-feminists, and then becoming after even more struggle lesbian-feminists-of-color (these hybridities were always present, of course, but for years remained invisible within the "minority" social bodies of feminism or African Americanism or Hispanic Americanism). The history of this particular struggle over the interminglings of minoritarian social bodies is entirely representative of the dilemmas facing the traditional political notion of identity politics grounded in a totalized, stable, and fixed subject. In a parallel though disjunct cultural scene, there is the instance of lesbians assimilating gay male sexual practices and the identities they mobilize—which San Francisco knows better than any other U.S. city. Such states of hybridity are made visible respectively by Audre Lorde's biomythography as a black-lesbian-feminist in *Zami* (1982) and Della Grace's photographs for a leather-lesbian identity politics in *Love Bites* (1991). In Grace's portrait of "Jane, Jane, Queen of Pain" we see a lesbian body appropriating the codes of straight porn while assimilating S/M sexual practices arising specifically out of the situationality of gay male bar culture.[16] Grace's images and Lorde's candid self-portrayal, along with all the other mass-produced representations of lesbian bodies currently circulating in popular culture, remind us of the ways in which lesbian bodies are crossed by multiplicitous regimes of signs.

Indeed, the potential power of lesbian identity politics in the current historical moment comes from its situatedness and alliances among feminist, gay male, and civil rights activisms. Some lesbian bodies are a current site of contention in the women's movement, particularly over the issue of S/M practices and porn, because of their greater affinities with gay males than with straight women. Furthermore, the activist politics of ACT-UP in the face of the ideological epidemic of significations surrounding AIDS represents for many lesbians a better strategy of cultural politics than the consciousness-raising discourses traditionally authorized by NOW. But in the face of direct losses on the ground gained in the 1960s, 1970s, and 1980s on women's issues—right to abortions and birth control information, right to protection from sexual harassment in the workplace, right to have recourse to a just law in the case of rape—the queer nation/straight feminism alliance will be crucial to the future of lesbian cultural politics.

This state of being lesbian in the age of postmechanical reproduction does not eradicate radical politics, but asks that we refigure our understanding of identity politics as a politics of transformation, hybridity, and flow as well as resistance, indeed a politics working from both inside and outside straight technoculture and the race and class structures that it reproduces. Haraway's "A Cyborg Manifesto" (1991) theorizes one direction that lesbians can mobilize for further developing alliance-based, unintegrated networks of power in the cultural game of identity politics. The strategy of making cyborg assemblages of bodies and technologies proposed by Haraway should have a special valence for lesbians, who as a group have a history of playing with body assemblages against which straight women's masqueradings pale by comparison.

If feminisms and Marxisms have run amok on Continental theoretical imperatives to construct a revolutionary subject that premises metaphysical identity closure, as Haraway (1991) argues, cyborg bodies, "stripped of identity," are free to rewrite the texts of their bodies and societies without the limit-texts of god/ man, self/other, culture/nature, m/f (176). Bearing the banner of subjects-as-etching-machines, cyborg politics would be the politics of multiplicitous coding practices and noise in a system of perfect communication, a politics of many in the place of one, of hybrids in the place of boundaries. For those who have experienced the dominations of the "autonomous" self, to etch the microsurfaces of the encoding social body as something less and more than a "One" may be an empowering reconceptualization of the "Family of Man."

Take camp struggles over straight semiosis, for example, which gay and lesbian subcultures have always understood as a style of everyday cultural politics and survival and not as prepolitical (a reading commonly produced by straight "politicized" subjects). If we premise that the body is not outside textuality, that the body is itself a field of signification, a site for the production of cultural meanings and ideological reifications, then one has to admit that you play the game this way or that, you choose to pass or not within this scene and the next, but you can't choose to stop playing with signs, with your own *material* production as a cultural (i.e., visibly signifying) body.

If we admit that social bodies exist only in a process of constant historical transformation, then there are only hybrid bodies, moving bodies, migrant bodies, becoming bodies, machinic-assemblage bodies. And in relation to bodies of signs in postindustrial capitalism, even in the case of the most organ-ized signifying regimes, Deleuze and Guattari (1987) insist there are only *trans*semiotics. It's futile then to ask what subjectivities *essentially* exist inside and alongside the transversed social bodies of postmodernity. Too many challenges facing lesbian cultural politics are rendered invisible by a discourse of essentialism. It is in this regard that Haraway's vision of unnatural, hyperconstructed social bodies in their potential, if blasphemous, positivity provides an empowering alternative strategy for thinking lesbian bodies and organ-izing lesbian cultural politics into a material (if monstrous) body of power. But thinking this circuited body that might order lesbian organs of power with and within other assemblages of identity and being will require not only Benjamin's critique of the state's technofetishization of technologies of reproduction, but Wittig's lesbian materialism, as well as Deleuze and Guattari's schizoanalysis of becoming under capitalism.

When we take up Haraway's cyborg project *for* lesbianism, for example, Wittig's essays on the political economy of lesbianism should remind us that the sites of political struggle over lesbian cyborg affinities will solidify around the historically and materially determined pragmatics of *who* gets to produce cyborg bodies, who has access, who provides the laboring and component bodies, and who becomes and who buys the commodities reproduced. If we accept that the body exists in an assemblage with technology, the "human" body itself may well appear subordinate to the cyborg body of which it is a part. Thus, cultural politics not only comes into conflict with the ideal of the totalized bourgeois subject, but comes into being encrypted in and by dominant signifying regimes of the state (such as media politics, the commodification of desires, New Reproductive Technologies, Star Wars, techno-progress, intelligence networks, and globalization). The problem of organ-ized agency will take on a dimensionality involving spatial and temporal coordinates of multi-plicitous, rhizomatic collective social "identities." In each case, we'd have to reconsider where a cyborg body begins and ends (the limits of the text), for example, or when an exteriority is also an interiority. And who will have ownership of the means of cyborg production and reproduction?

Lesbian bodies are not essentially counterhegemonic sites of culture, as Wittig (1992) might like to theorize. The lesbian may not be a woman, as she argues in "One Is Not Born a Woman," yet she is not entirely exterior to straight culture. Each lesbian has a faciality touching on some aspect of a majority signifying regime of postmodernity, whether that be masculinity/femininity, motherhood, race or the nation-state, the sex industry, technologies of simulation, surgical techno-plasties, the commodification of selves and knowledges, reproductive technologies, or the military under global capitalism. Lesbians are inside and outside, minority and majority, *at the same time*.

Lesbian bodies have always presented a challenge to essentialist notions of feminine identity, and never more so than when lesbians are set in the historical context of postmodernity. The cultural period in late industrial and postindustrial society during World War II and in the fifty years since is their historical heyday. Lesbian bodies came of age under the spectre of a Holocaust that could reach finality only by the injection into the global symbolic of a nuclear sublime so horrific as to arrest all prior signification. Their agencies must be agencies that work with the reduced political rights of a worldwide civilian population under the new military regime of global security (Virilio). They are proffered a variety of prostheses and self-imaging technologies, in fact, a variety of bodies, as long as they meet the performativity criterion of commodity logic. And if they are runaways, they're running from the very political economy that produced their possibility. This is their double bind. For all these reasons, the immediate challenge facing lesbian bodies in postmodernity is how to make a dis-organ-ized body of signs and identities work for a progressive, or even a radical, politics.

THREE

Becoming War-Machine

Depredatory: destructive, consuming, wasteful, deleterious; that preys upon other animals:

creature of prey and its organs of capture.

> Depredate: to prey upon, make prey of, to consume by waste.

> Depredation: the action of making prey of, plundering, ravaging;

consumption or destructive waste of the substance of anything; destructive operations.

> Depredator: one who, or that which, preys upon or makes

depredations, a plunderer; one who lays waste.

—Oxford English Dictionary

The image of women who kill has taken on in the contemporary public imaginary in the United States a particularly symptomatic inflection, one entirely paradigmatic of breakdowns in the sex-gender system produced by women's relations to a depredatory machinic organization in the twentieth century. In the next few chapters, I map the flows of becoming-woman in relation to depredatory systems in postindustrial society. My first entry point into the problematic of a feminine depredatory machine is the systematic recruitment, incorporation, and regulation of women by the U.S. military.[1] My working assumption is that the new predatory function of the feminine does not mark the emergence of an aberration of gender but rather signs a symptomatology of "normative" femininities emerging within late capitalism.

The "war-machine," by which I mean all those practices surrounding the military and its organization of strategic, tactical, and manpower resources, is altering the very definition of the feminine as a set of gendered social roles. Military practices, both within the United States and at foreign military bases, are not only shaping gendered race relations, but are also forming the latest obstacle to transnational feminist movements. One can see this by mapping the relations among women within the war-machine, that is, the relations of women to each other, because doing so reveals a sacrificial economy that makes some women predators and depredators while marking other women as sacrificial bodies.

In the month of January 1996, the Fourth World Conference on Women published a statement in the *New York Times* calling for the peace-loving people of the United States and the world to remove all 136 U.S. military bases from Japan and to ban all testing and manufacture of nuclear weapons (*New York Times*, January 26, 1996, A11). This statement was made in response to the abduction and brutal rape of a twelve-year-old Okinawan schoolgirl by three U.S. servicemen (two navy seamen and one marine). The U.S. media attention given to this event was not due to the unusualness of the violence. On the same day that these three servicemen were prosecuted, in fact, another marine was sentenced to eleven years in prison for repeatedly punching an Okinawan woman in the head until she died, after he had had an argument with her (*Pittsburgh Post Gazette*, January 30, 1996, A4). Rather, the media attention was the result of the organized efforts of the Fourth World Conference on Women to publicize the event. The Conference Action Program brought together in collective protest the Japan Housewives Association, Women Religious Workers in Japan, the Japan Christian Temperence Union, the National Women's Council, the Federation of Japanese Women's Organizations, and the New Japan Women's Association, as well as various high-profile women writers, artists, and intellectuals. While Japanese women appealed to the peace-loving people of the world to remove U.S. military bases and thus stop such recurrent violence against Japanese women, however, women in the United States were joining the military in ever increasing rates, and requesting and winning the right to serve in combat, in a politics of equivalency in which women demand the same rights as men.

This situation marks a significant break from past feminist antiwar politics, such as those enacted by the collective Women Strike for Peace in the early 1960s. In 1962, at the end of its reign of power, the House Un-American Activities Committee subpoenaed thirteen peace activists from the collective to "determine the extent of Communist Party infiltration into the peace movement" (Swerdlow 8). Many historians credit Women Strike for Peace with striking the final blow in the fall of the House Un-American Activities Committee in a dramatic standoff between "national security needs" and the moral claims of women as life-bearers to oppose war (Swerdlow 8). The feminist counter-use of traditional sex role ideology allowed feminists to claim their rights as women and as mothers "to influence the course of government" toward peace and nonmilitary development. Ironically, by 1992, only thirty years later, the right to serve in the military had become the latest sign in the United States of a woman's full civil rights.

The sex-gender system once provided exemption for women from immediate participation in a ritualized or state killing-machine—from ritual sacrifice in ancient Aztec culture to military organizations in modernity—except, of course, as sacrificial or civilian victims or as part of support mechanisms such as intelligence gathering, data processing, supply transport, medical aid, and military wifehood—not to mention prostitution for "R & R."[2] The Aquino government estimated 25,000 women "entertainment workers" in Olongapo City alone, home of Subic Bay Naval base, which closed in 1991 after Marcos's fall from power and after years of local and national protest against the United States's military presence in the Philippines (Enloe 86). I am not suggesting, therefore, that women have not participated indirectly in a killing-machine throughout the centuries, through all the ways in which they complied with, or were forced to comply with, regimes of state power that depend upon regimes of violence in order to operate. Indeed, the first military computers in the late nineteenth century were rooms full of women operating calculators, carrying out the large-scale computations needed for ballistic analysis (De Landa 1991, 41). But prior to the mid-twentieth century, women were exempted from the killing fields.

This chapter approaches the problematic of the feminine becoming war-machine by deploying Deleuze and Guattari's notion of machinic, or metallic, phylum. Deleuze and Guattari define machinic phylum as "the flow of matter-movement... in continuous variation" (1987, 406). This matter-flow and the consciousness it imposes upon matters and operations is "essentially metallic or metallurgical," in the sense that metallurgy opened onto a "morphogenetic lineage" in which thresholds of qualitative transformations of matter overspill "incarnated forms" (410). In that electricity is a result of the conductive properties of metals, the metallurgical phylum is the foundation of machine culture and electronic culture. The phylum traverses matter at various levels, from flows of turbulence at the level of physics, to chains of processes at the chemical level, to potential thresholds in biological systems. The machinic phylum's relation to turbulent and self-organizing behavior in social systems is currently an area of theoretical speculation, not only by poststructuralist social theorists such as Deleuze and Guattari, De Landa, Ronell, and Virilio, but also by the Pentagon, in the form of mathematical modeling techniques providing algorithms for war simulations and for "nonfirepower driven" scenarios, such as "the impact of AIDS on the stability of Third World governments" (De Landa 57, 20).

Self-organizing singularities of the machinic phylum within social systems are determined by the interface of morphogenetic flows of matter-energy and forces of social turbulence that are channeled into human technologies and human processes of culture (Deleuze and Guattari 406). Turbulence can be generated by any number of factors, including abrupt or gradual demographic shifts stimulated by birthrates, food supply, war, natural catastrophe, disease, as well as by transportation, communication, and medical technologies. While social turbulence can affect the self-organizing properties of the machinic phylum in any number of ways, the singular properties of the machinic phylum are in turn capable of generating social turbulence and reorganization. For example, gas lighting is a component part of the architectural space of the modern factory, out of which emerges the subject position of the factory worker in the early nineteenth century (Schivelbusch 1988). Similarly, the train and telegraph determine the substance of expression of nineteenth-century mercantile expansion as much as mercantile expansion determined the form of expression of the imperialist train-telegraph assemblage (Schivelbusch 1986). In World War II, tactical innovations such as the blitzkrieg resulted from the assemblage of tanks, aircraft, and FM radio with the abstract machine of nationalism and its concrete mechanisms of militarist expansion (Kittler).

According to De Landa (1991), who has applied the concept of the machinic phylum to the analysis of military history, human epigenetic processes, resulting from cultural practices, put pressures on matter and species to accelerate adaption toward human requirements, producing changes "100 to 1000 times faster than genetic evolutionary processes at the species level" (39). At the same time, however, morphogenetic lineages (self-organizations of matter-energy flow and their emergent properties in an interface with human technologies and cultural practices) also put pressures on the human species to adapt toward machinic requirements (i.e., the rationalization of labor, including the rationalization of the social bodies that provide component parts for human-machinic assemblages organizing the social). De Landa defines the machinic phylum more generally

to refer both to processes of self-organization in general and to the particular assemblages in which the power of these processes may be integrated. . . . In one sense, the term refers to any population (of atoms, molecules, cells, insects) whose global dynamics are determined by singularities (bifurcations and attractors); in another sense, it refers to the integration of a collection of elements into an assemblage that is more than the sum of its parts, that is, one that displays global properties not possessed by its individual components. (20)

De Landa's reading, following Deleuze and Guattari's, both de-instrumentalizes technology, displacing the traditional hierarchy that subordinates it to human intentionality, and reconfigures the space of the social subject. In an interview with Andrew Payne (1992), De Landa defined "machinic phylum" as "the ability which flows of matter and energy have to spontaneously generate order out of chaos. In many cases this creative capability of 'mere' matter-energy flows results in the spontaneous assembly of machine-like structures" (128).[3]

As De Landa points out, such a de-instrumentalized theory of self-organization in regard, first, to matter-energy, and, second, to the human assembly of these phenomena as technologies inscribed within specific cultural practices, bears implications for any materialist philosophy of the future.[4] In addition, the theory of self-organization articulated in the notion of the machinic phylum points to the need to theorize collective social identities together with human technologies as being themselves the working parts of larger human-machinic assemblages.

The notion of becoming-machinic, then, suggests both the ways in which human social bodies are integrated into a culture's global dynamics and the particular component roles these bodies may play within a given human-machinic assemblage. Becoming *killing-machine* suggests the ways in which human-machinic assemblages organize and regulate predatory and sacrificial functions within culture or between cultures, as well as the ways in which social bodies are inscribed and rationalized according to those functions.

State reterritorializations of the feminine in postmodern cultural formations, and the stakes of those reterritorializations, cannot be adequately calculated without some attempt to map the breakdowns occurring in this contemporary collision course between the two concurrent yet distinct cultural flows of becoming-woman and becoming-depredatory. This chapter maps the dynamics of that collision in regard to the military's accession of female substitute bodies precisely at a time when the state is in contention with women over abortion practices and combat status, while the military's advanced research groups are, as De Landa points out, removing humans from the "decision-making loop" of advanced predatory weapons systems.[5]

Well into the twentieth century, the predatory position was historically thought of as ultimately and exclusively masculine. Exceptions in history, such as Joan of Arc, were aberrations (an act of God) that appeared sporadically and typically had to be sacrificed once their tactical use had been served. By World War I, however, women in the United States were being identified as acceptable substitute bodies for tasks close to, if not yet at the center of, predatory functions, in the wake of the tremendous drain on the male youth population incurred by twentieth-century technologies of warfare. By World War II, women were being both systematically incorporated within the war-machine of the late-modern nation-state and carefully regulated to remain exterior to the predatory core of it — through their exclusion from fighter-pilot, warship, and ground-troop combat status as well as through recruitment ceilings. Still, women were becoming more and more during the twentieth century an indispensable if problematic component of the war-machine, one requiring both programs of recruitment and strategies for containment. Military recruitment of U.S. women in World War II through the Women's Army Corps, for example, exempted women from combat exposure and relegated them to support functions in order to free the primary labor of male soldiers. Similarly, the Women's Air Force Service Pilots Program, initiated in November 1942, supplied substitute female pilots for support functions in order to free male pilots for the front only during the worst years of pilot shortage, and the program was deactivated when male pilots returned from the Western front in December 1944 (Cole 1992).

In spite of various gender limitations institutionalized by the military itself, the demand for substitute bodies produced a turbulent flow of women into the war-machine during the course of the twentieth century. China after the Maoist revolution incorporated women into the military, even at the level of ground infantry, as did the post-world war Israeli state in the 1948 War of Independence, as did the Eritrean resistance in Ethiopia. In the Persian Gulf War in 1991, 35,000 U.S. women served behind the front lines. And in May 1991, the U.S. House of Representatives voted to permit the Air Force, Navy, and Marine Corps to use women as combat pilots. Shortly thereafter, the U.S. Senate Armed Services Subcommittee began hearing arguments for permitting women to enter ground combat. In April 1993, Defense Secretary Les Aspin ordered the military services to drop any remaining restrictions on women in aerial and naval combat as part of President Clinton's "first one hundred days program." On April 28, the day of the Pentagon's announcement, national newspaper headlines declared "Women Will Go to Combat" flying fighter and bomber planes, carrier-based planes, and Apache helicopter gunships amidst debate over "conditions for the use of force in Bosnia." Whereas women were never more than 2 percent of the military in World War II, since the institution of an all-volunteer force in the United States in 1973, the percentage of women serving on active duty in the military has increased to nearly 12 percent (Palmer 1991; Center for Defense Information 1995). And while the U.S. Supreme Court upheld the exclusion of women from the draft in *Rostker v. Goldberg* in 1981, demographic projections suggest that the pool of draft-age males will continue to decline throughout the 1990s (Jones 1990).

It is not surprising in regard to this demographic flow of women into the armed services, and in regard to the social turbulence such a demographic flow is capable of generating, that the tendency of contemporary armed forces is toward channeling female personnel into the middle ranks, where they serve as middle management. In the U.S. military in 1995, women made up 12.7 percent of the commissioned officer corps—though, not surprisingly, the number of female commissioned officers decreases as one ascends the grade scale (Center for Defense Information 1995).[6] By 1994, there were no female generals or admirals, ten female brigadier generals and lower rear admirals, and 12,908 female captains and lieutenants (Department of Defense, Table 10). By 1995, women made up 11.9 percent of total enlisted personnel, with more women channeled into the noncommissioned officer corps than the most junior positions, such as ground troops (Center for Defense Information).[7] This containment pattern, which has channeled women away from both top-ranking leadership and ground troop assignments, has generated a particular form of social and semiotic turbulence: the emergence of the heroic, "charismatic" feminine leader and her contradictions. This variation of the traditional military leadership model premises the subordinate soldiers' identification with their revered leader, the physical and moral ascendency of the leader, and the emotional bonding of the group.

The gender contradictions of charismatic military leadership in women creates a certain instability in the gendered social function which military service has traditionally provided, that is, initiation into masculinity. The female military leader is both a deterritorialization of state forms of militarized masculinity and a state reterritorialization of militarized femininities. While it is possible to imagine positive change resulting from disseminating feminine gender characteristics into the military's pyramidal-hierarchical organization and leadership styles, and while various military journals have praised the emergence of the charismatic female leader among female noncommissioned and commissioned officers (Boulègue), it's also clear that the military has always functioned as a cultural site of masculine socialization, and will continue to do so whether the human bodies it assimilates are male or female. Thus, at the same time that we are witnessing a deterritorialization of the military's social initiation into masculinity as it recruits women, we also see masculinity and its military rite of passage being systematically reterritorialized onto substitute female initiates.

The contradiction manifested by women's assimilation into leadership roles within the military hierarchy has not gone unnoticed by the mainstream film industry, which has produced blockbusters capitalizing on the anxieties stirred by militarized and masculinized feminine bodies and by a potentially femininized war machine. *The Terminator* (1984) and *Terminator 2: Judgment Day* (1991) series, for example, not only presented film audiences with a sci-fi screen projection of a future, muscle-bound paramilitary woman who happens to be a mother and to participate in military roles traditionally defining masculine identity—fighting and commanding—but also images the promethean transformation of that screen body from suburban femininity in *T-1* to paramilitary in *T-2*. In *The Terminator*, the female protagonist played by Linda Hamilton is constructed on the late modern myth of the feminine political rebel—what Sarah Connor will become one day in the future though there is no sign of this incorporeal transformation in the banality of her life in the present. The narrative function of the feminine in this mythos is actually quite traditional—to birth and rear the future revolutionary male resistance leader, John Connor, who, like Sarah, could be anyone white and middle class. In this regard, *The Terminator* is a perfect 1980s antiabortion film. In *Terminator 2*, however, the extraordinary extent of muscle development in Linda Hamilton's screen body—which competed on its own terms with Arnold Schwarzenegger's (Hamilton's weight training regimen for the film is now legendary among women bodybuilders)—challenged long-standing social assumptions about the physiological limitations of women's "strength" in combat.

The *Alien* series—*Alien* (1979), *Aliens* (1986), and *Alien*[3] (1992)—follows a similar but more socially contentious trajectory, presenting Sigourney Weaver as a sci-fi version of a self-possessed, right-to-choice mother and charismatic military leader who becomes increasingly masculinized as the series proceeds. The character, Ridley, is raped by the alien in the final film of the series—a rape threatened but never actualized in the first two *Alien* films. Because she is in deep-space sleep at the time of the violation, the rape conveniently occurs before the final film's narrative enters screen-time, though we are provided later with a virtual rape scene that helps us to imaginatively fill in the missing primal scene that drives the narrative. Ridley must either choose a double killing in the form of suicide-feticide (a screen trace of a desperate and fatal self-abortion) or provide the substitute womb for capital's reproduction of the ultimate military product—a virtually indestructable biotech predator. She chooses a fatal self-abortion, but not before taking command of a crew of hardened and disgruntled criminals—mostly black and all male—through a spectacular display of sheer Weberian grace.

The linear progression of the film's narrative reveals Ridley's leadership to be grounded in moral and technical superiority rather than coercion, in spite of the structural contradiction within the narrative's opening sequence, which makes it quite clear that the men she leads are prisoners subjected to forced labor within a system that operates by coercive power. Ridley is on the surface a liminal figure who can operate as leader because she is seemingly outside the darkly satiric mise-en-scène in which the film sets the alien as fantasmatic bio-weapon turned phallic nightmare. In this degenerate military-industrial-labor network, individual bodies become nothing more than component parts for the productive and reproductive functions of the vastly complex, integrated predatory systems of postmodern capital. Yet, structurally, Ridley embodies traditional masculine military behavior and values of leadership—an embodiment visually conveyed in the character's strikingly masculine appearance in the final film. The tension that drives the filmic narrative is the same tension described by one historian in regard to contemporary French military society, which deploys conscription, as "participation—minority and subordinate—in the leadership of armed forces that are almost exclusively male and mostly recruited by coercive means" (Boulègue 345).

In the United States, tensions between junior male enlisted ranks and noncommissioned female officers are somewhat alleviated by the cessation of conscription since 1973. Yet the turbulence of these gender relations within the armed services, in which white women serve in middle management while women and men of color serve in lower level and ground troop positions, is hardly eliminated by an all-volunteer corps. Even without an active draft, demographic distribution of gender within the ranks is clearly complicated by racial distribution.

Between 1974 and 1989, the percentage of enlisted African Americans increased from 15 to 23 percent, while black men composed a greater proportion of junior enlisted ranks than whites in the army (Moore 363). From the end of the Vietnam War to the end of the 1980s, the percentage of African American women in the military increased sixfold, reaching 33.7 percent by 1989 and yielding a military accession rate three times greater than that of white women (3.7 of every 1,000 black women enlists to 1.3 of every 1,000 white women). Furthermore, Department of Defense statistics for 1987 showed black women between the ages of 18 and 21 underwent military accession at a substantially higher rate than black men in the same age group, while black men already made up a greater proportion of junior enlisted ranks than whites in the army (Moore 363–64). By 1992, though black women in the United States composed only 12 percent of the total population, they made up 48.7 percent of all enlisted women in the army (Enloe 1993, 84–87).

In spite of these increases, African American women constituted just 13.2 percent of all female officers in 1989, and only 20.2 percent of all army officers in 1994 (Moore; Stiehm 271–72; Enloe 1993, 84–87). Thus, while the corps of noncommissioned white women officers continued to swell particularly in the highly technical organizations (such as the air force), junior enlisted ranks in the lowest technical military organization (the army) were filled with African American men serving as ground troops and African American women assigned to low-level technical occupations in administration and support—the first occupations likely to be phased out in the event of cutbacks.

This situation is dramatized in *Alien*[3] by the narrative necessity for a white woman to establish military leadership over a group of angry, discontented underclass black men who are conscripted as laboring bodies by state coercion. The conflict driving *Alien*[3] dramatizes the predicament of the female noncommissioned officer, who is, not surprisingly, white. This predicament is resolved in the film by displaced group aggression on an enemy "alien," white female and minority male teamwork (with the white woman contributing technical knowledge and organization skills and the minority males contributing labor), and feminine martyrdom. The narrative bears an uncanny correlation to actual demographic flows into the post–World War II military corps. Clearly, the channeling and regulating of feminine bodies into the war-machine inscribe a set of class-specific and race-specific social investments in a state military-industrial system that includes not only the military proper, but also its industrial-labor extensions in research and development within the university[8] and in business, aerospace recruitment, mass production and "global" marketing of war technologies, as well as management practices based on military models and privileging prior military service, particularly for noncommissioned officers.

It is difficult to predict the outcomes of these confluences, but the sites of social turbulence they are producing are glaringly clear. Live births in the

United States fell dramatically in the late 1960s — the end of the "baby boomer" generation, which began in 1945 — while legal abortions in the United States increased from 740,000 in 1973 (the first year of legalized abortion) to over 1.5 million from 1985 through the early 1990s (Rodman 23–26; U.S. Bureau of the Census 81). These abortion practices, occurring at the same time as popularization of contraception with the pill, exacerbated an already diminishing pool of male bodies for military accession in the 1980s and 1990s. The pool of able-bodied men will continue to diminish into the next century if this pattern is not altered, increasing the military's need for substitute bodies (a need currently reaching a crisis point in aerospace recruitment) and the need to coordinate birthrates and cultural practices of abortion and contraception with the late-modern nation-state's military-industrial-labor network.

At the same time that women are being reterritorialized by the military, however, the military accession of women threatens to deterritorialize the masculine system of hierarchies on which the military operates, as well as the long-established sexual division of labor between masculine predatory functions and maternal functions of reproduction. Women now serve both gender functions — doubling duties to the state that were once gender-divided. While war once seemed as masculine as maternity was feminine, the sex that gives life is now also the sex that kills. It is not surprising that this breakdown of the traditional division of sex roles is asymmetrical in regard to gender: "Motherhood remains the symbol of femininity while masculinity is losing its symbolic meaning — in war as in the world of work" (Boulègue 347). Furthermore, gendered racial inequalities can be expected to increase between African American males in the junior enlisted ranks in the Army and the growing corps of white women noncommissioned officers, particularly as recruitment quotas for women rise in all the services in relation to the need for more substitute bodies. In the event of a return to conscription, this inequality could be expected to fuel popular male sentiment for including female citizens in the draft — as it already has in France (Boulègue 350).

Perhaps the most disturbing film to give formal expression to a nightmare screen projection of woman-in-the-integrated-predatory-circuit was Luc Besson's *La Femme Nikita* (1991), a French production that circulated widely in the United States via the home video market and which spurred a poor American imitation entitled *Point of No Return* in 1992. *Nikita* forwent science-fiction dystopia for an unrelenting realism set to reverberate between everyday contemporary French culture and the inner workings of the late modern state's central intelligence network. In this film, the working-class female outlaw-protagonist acquires simultaneously both masculine predatory skills and class-inscribed feminine skills of sexual attractiveness as a trained assassin working for the state intelligence agency in covert operations. The film creates a now common end-of-the-century screen nightmare—the feminized predator—at the same time that it makes masculinity and femininity visible as concrete processes of acculturation. Nikita is a postmodern Pygmalion—a body programmed within an abstract intelligence machine. Her character challenges the myth of nonviolence as a feminine characteristic. The performance by actress Anne Parillaud and direction by Besson are shocking in regard to the character's physical prowess and skilled handling of an assortment of handguns, long-range rifles, silencers, assault weapons, champagne glasses, eye makeup, high heels, evening dresses, salad forks, and so on. The psychological and emotional crux of the film's tortuous two hours of tension is Nikita's assignment to assassinate an unidentified political figure who turns out, at the last instant, to be a woman. Nikita completes the assignment while her male lover tries to seduce her through the locked bathroom door. Merely a component part of a state-organized killing-machine, taking orders from an intelligent system without a face, Nikita emblematizes the function of woman as component body in a coercive and violent system she has neither created nor chosen. Besson's representation of feminine violence is antinostalgic—at the film's opening and before her Promethean transformation, Nikita is little more than an animal living on the fringes of the socius—a lower-class drug addict with a serious death drive, who in cold blood shoots a policeman in the face at point-blank range. Nikita's strategic social reprogramming emblematizes the military's function as a socialization tool and regulation machine for the underclasses, a machine that functions not only in regard to women, but also in regard to gays and lesbians who are recruited as closeted and then policed rather than actually refused entrance into the system,[9] while both male and female lower-class blacks are heavily recruited by the Army and then disproportionately channeled into low-status jobs (i.e., nontechnical jobs). Though in the end Nikita flees her role in the intelligence network, she finds herself, like the female heroes of *Alien*³ and *Terminator 2*, on the run with no previolent or nonviolent social space to return to.

   Beyond Hollywood's screen projections, the actual possibilities for women to reterritorialize masculine violence and values in the process of military initiation or, worse, in actual combat, are quite constrained.[10] Popular filmic representations of militarized women hardly correspond to the actual experiences of servicewomen. Take the case of one of the first women to qualify as a fighter pilot for the U.S. military (in 1996 there were 8 women fighter pilots compared to 4,448 men). Jackie Parker learned to fly before she learned to drive and became an Air Force Pilot by the age of twenty. She was the youngest spaceflight air traffic controller at NASA, first woman Air Force test pilot, and youngest woman to serve as an instructor pilot on a variety of aircraft. In the summer of 1995, she resigned from military service. Assigned to a squadron nicknamed "the boys from Syracuse," she suffered constant harassment during a training program that stretched out for over two hundred hours when male pilots often passed through in twenty. According to an investigation that later verified her charges of harassment, one fellow pilot joked about shooting Parker in the stomach "so she would die a slow death" (*Sun Sentinel*, January 9, 1996, E1).

Or consider the experience of U.S. Army Captain Linda Bray, who had troops under fire at three locations in Panama at the time of the U.S. invasion in 1990. Bray became a media figure because of her gender status as the "first woman in combat." Later, she held that the media attention caused the military hierarchy to "cold shoulder" her into a medical discharge by transferring the soldiers in her company and submitting the entire unit to an Army Criminal Investigation, though it found no evidence against Bray or her company and she was later exonerated (Copeland).

Or consider the scandal over the 1991 Tailhook Association annual convention in the Las Vegas Hilton. The Tailhook convention is an annual event for naval officers that, while only unofficially affiliated with the navy, was supported with navy funding. The federal investigation following the scandal found ninety occurrences of molestation and indecent assault by naval officers; 117 officers were implicated in incidents of indecent assault, indecent exposure, conduct unbecoming an officer, or failure to act in a proper leadership capacity (Office of the Inspector General, 2). The "gauntlet of TH91" was witnessed by Vice Admiral Richard Dunleavy, assistant chief of Naval Operations, but he took no action at the time. The gauntlet consisted of a hallway on the third floor lined by drinking naval officers who funneled women down the hall when they exited the elevator. Indecent assaults that occurred in the gauntlet included stripping off women's clothes from the waist down and passing them overhead, punching women who resisted in the face, butt biting, indecent exposure of the testicles, and verbal harassment (50, 52, 61). Admiral Kelso, chief of Naval Operations, later stated, "Tailhook brought to light the fact that we had an institutional problem with women" (ix).

One navy officer during the investigation compared Tailhook to the common practice of a "cruise party":

Well, I don't think it's any secret that in times in the past, after we've been at sea for a long time and we've gone into port for the first time in some amount of time at sea, that we—that,

traditionally, Navy aviation sets up an admin suite, what we call an admin suite in a hotel.
And this is normally a common suite where guys can meet. It's kind of
our living room ashore for a brief period of time.

A lot of times it seems to serve two functions: It's one place where we can all congregate, and at other
times it's a place of pretty—some good parties. You know, when I say the word "party"
I mean somewhat similar—somewhat along the lines of what was happening up at Tailhook....
Well this tradition of doing this on cruise is exactly what the suite thing at Tailhook is.
It's the same thing. There's no difference, really, between the two. (32)

The Tailhook experience sums up the contradiction facing U.S. women joining the military. What was considered "normal," acceptable behavior with foreign women in port at military bases in Korea, the Philippines, and Japan, belies a pervasive sexist attitude toward women in general that is reproduced in military culture. The only reason Tailhook was a scandal at all was that so many of the women assaulted during that convention were themselves naval officers.

It is important to note, furthermore, that the cultural debate over the role of women in the military is occurring precisely at a time when the military-industrial-labor complex is channeling the phylogenic lineages of organic materials, social bodies, and machinic organizations toward autonomous predatory weapons systems and tactical intelligence systems. TENCAP (Tactical Exploitation of National Capabilities) organizes satellite and computer technologies to render radar an offensive weapon as part of a Control, Command, Communications, and Intelligence (C^3I) network capable of bypassing national intelligence to send information directly and immediately to forces in the field (De Landa 56). The Pentagon also announced in a "Strategic Computing" document plans for applications of artificial intelligence in expert systems technology such as "battle management advisers" and "cockpit advisers" (De Landa 171).

As this machinic threshold between strategic intelligence and tactical intelligence is successfully accomplished, the military rationalization of labor will pass into an entirely new phase—and whether or not women comprise part of the corp of ground troops, combat pilots, or noncommissioned officers will matter very little in the execution of strategico-tactical decision making. Likewise, the state-appropriated war machine's advances in solving the technical problems of complexity management, parallel processing, and real-time satellite data transmission, and its investments in intelligent machines (AI), in technological control of the electromagnetic spectrum (Star Wars), and in removing humans from the decision-making loop in nonhuman intelligent weapons systems, render questions about the feminization of the military increasingly moot. Unmanned missiles, armed logical robot sentries such as the PROWLER (Programmable Robot Observer with Logical Enemy Response), and strategic computing systems are creating Control, Command, Communications, and Intelligence networks that are more and more independent of human input and control (De Landa 160, 170).

This logic has had very concrete effects on women's relation to warfare. While *La Femme Nikita* showed viewing audiences the nightmare of a woman killing another woman in the form of a paramilitary female assassin turned against a white female member of the bourgeoisie, the reality of depredatory relations among women is again more racially stratified. War photography, unlike the film industry, too often reveals the enemy's face in actual warfare to be the face of the racially othered woman. This is because the percentage of civilian casualties out of total war casualties has risen from 14 percent in World War I to over 90 percent in the 1990s (United Nations International Children's Emergency Fund). The reasons for this rise are not only changes in military technologies, but also the ideology of "just war" discourse in which civilians—whether men, women, or children in the civilian population—are not the reference point in "strategic defense," "global security," and "just war" simulations. Rather, the weapons themselves and analogic simulations of "the calculus of gain and loss" have taken precedence (Cohn 34, Elshtain). In such discourse, in which the news media function as a window by which we police ourselves through the constant threat of pandemonium,[11] human bodies are rationalized as tool-bodies, target-bodies, or "calculated losses" in various weapons systems scenarios.

The movement toward militarizing women in the United States is irreversible. Feminine investments in the war-machine and its military-industrial-labor complex are extensive. Furthermore, the accelerating accession rate of lower-income African American women by the armed services and the channeling of them disproportionately into low-status positions with little room for career advancement while white women are recruited as noncommissioned officers reproduces oppressive race relations. And in becoming militarized, the women's movement at large has lost an effective and powerful counter-use of traditional sex role ideology once so crucial to the peace movement—the right of women as life-bearers and caretakers to pressure governments toward peace and nonmilitary development.[12] Acting on a 1973 Brookings Institution study that argued that military recruitment of women would relieve manpower shortages accompanying the end of the draft and would do so in a cost-effective way because women were less expensive to recruit than men, the military strategically increased quotas for women in the corps from 2 percent in

1973 to nearly 12 percent by 1995 (Schultze 148–49). To date, women have participated actively in offensive U.S. military missions against Granada in 1983, Libya in 1986, Panama in 1989, and Iraq in 1991 (Becraft). Any redress of this accelerating accession pattern channeling women into the state-appropriated war-machine would involve the extensive development of an alternative economy large enough to compete with the resources of the current military economy. That would mean not only competing to create jobs as good as those provided by direct military service, but also competing for labor within the entire military-industrial-labor complex, including defense-oriented university research.

Obviously, an economic transition of this magnitude is nowhere on the horizon. In the meantime, women in the military have interfaced with computerized radar technologies to shoot down Scud missiles with "Patriots," transported gasoline and ammunition to frontline troops, flown supply planes into combat zones, and died, during Desert Storm (Gross, Randolph). After Desert Storm's "victory" in 1991 (a victory verified by all forms of U.S. military strategical calculations yet remaining in January 1993 still "unacknowledged" by Saddam Hussein as Bush departed office amid a flurry of last-minute cruise missile attacks against Iraq), female officers appeared before the U.S. Senate Armed Services Subcommittee to support assigning women to frontline ground combat duty. One month later, the Senate approved two controversial provisions while moving toward passage of a $291 billion defense authorization bill for fiscal year 1992 that included repeal of a 1948 law excluding women from flying in combat and a modified Strategic Defense Initiative plan authorizing $4.6 billion of the $5.2 billion requested by the Bush administration for deployment of a new antiballistic missile system and Brilliant Pebbles space-based defenses (Gilmartin). Other items up for action at the same time as the Senate hearings on women's future role in the military — $245 million for the rail garrison MX and $34 million for the new Short Range Attack Missile-Tactical.

The militarization of women since World War II exemplifies the collision course between social institutionalizations of predatory-machinic functions and the reproduction of "normative" feminine social functions in postmodern culture. The argument for "equivalency for women in the military" is a reification of the systematic accession of feminine substitute bodies as component parts for a structurally white male state-appropriated war-machine that must, by definition, regularly prey on "others" and colonize hierarchies of "others" to continue to expand its markets (i.e., the global multinational military-industrial-labor-investment banking complex that has emerged in postmodernity, rationalized by a discourse of "global security" and commodity logic, and always only partially appropriated by the state as such).[13] As military technologies advance, they must be channeled and regulated to keep the soldier a tool rather than a decision-making subject, controlling technologies' double-edged sword by turning the progression of technology inward toward interior surveillance even as the space of that interiority expands outward to the stratosphere. At every point at which the decision-making body proliferates, it must also police itself, replacing whenever possible individual human decision-making with networked computer memory banks and artificial command structures. In the process of becoming militarized, women are (en)trained with a skill, taught to be "all they can be" as technician, tool, and component body for a global decision-making system designed to freeze individual commands and to rationalize itself by the constant threat of pandemonium that it helps create.

F O U R

"Feticidal" Attractors

Demographic Turbulence

In addition to the pressures placed on the social process of becoming-woman by the state-appropriated war machine and its military-industrial economies, the social functions of the feminine are being deterritorialized, and reterritorialized, by the channeling of the machinic phylum into medical technologies and practices. Perhaps the most destabilizing of these social practices is abortion. Legal abortion in the United States had reached a state of normalization and public visibility by 1985 (more than 1.5 million abortions per year and holding steadily at that rate through 1992) to the extent that it began to threaten traditional gendered social structures regulating the reproduction of power, from declining WASP marriage rates and birthrates to the reproduction of mothering as a normative feminine social role (Rodman 24; U.S. Bureau of the Census 81). Throughout the 1980s and early 1990s, abortion practices had generated enough social turbulence to evoke a systematic challenge from both the federal and state court systems during Reagan and Bush's three Republican terms of office.

The dynamics of the machinic phylum at the level of the social shaped the substance and form of expression of abortion as a historically specific cultural practice in the United States. Abortion as we understand it today results from an assemblage of factors, including antibiotic properties, surgical technologies (specifically, vacuum aspiration perfected on the war front in Vietnam), baby boomer demographics, the "sexual revolution," the women's movement, and civil rights litigation concerning the right to privacy. The interface between human reproduction and the material practices of medical science has always been a site of political struggle between masculine and feminine orders in culture.[1] If at times the outcomes of this merger between a masculine machinic and a maternal organic have been liberating for women, at other times the results have been manifestly ominous. From the time the medical profession assimilated birth practices under its jurisdiction in the eighteenth century, reterritorializing it from the feminine domain of midwifery, medical advances in the engineering of life went hand in hand with the engineering of death. Male doctors in Germany, learning anatomy under the new teaching practice of cadaver dissection before the widespread standardization of Lister's antiseptic sterilization procedures published in 1867, brought to the scene of birth the rewards of scientific medicine as a plague of maternal deaths from postpartum bacterial infections carried on the contaminated hands of male practitioners (Rickels 313).

Modern allopathic practices in the West resulted from channeling the machinic phylum through the abstract-machine of empirical science and commodity logic. As a result, modern medicine brought to the scene of reproduction not only the scientific method but the reification of the maternal relation. In a process of translating social relations into object relations characteristic of instrumental reason, the mother and child became a series of "object-things" (Taussig 96). These object-things, such as the mother as "pregnant patient" or later "pregnant uterus," the child as "fetus," and life as "viability," could then be subject to the analytic and empirical methods of science. These methods shaped the therapeutic properties of organic chemicals (anesthesia), biological processes (bacterial sterilization, antibiotics, fertility drugs, and contraceptives), and machinic qualities (surgical instruments, vacuum aspirators, diagnostic and imaging machines).

Biomedicine's reterritorializations of the feminine body and its reproductive organs affect in some way all fields of the social. The machinic engineering of human reproduction generates reterritorializations along two strata—one organic and one machinic. On one level, medical technologies channel the machinic phylum in order to control biological reproduction (e.g., the pill, in vitro fertilization, abortion). On another level, the biological body and human biomass are subject to machinic properties (e.g., the imposition of corporate career schedules onto reproduction). This double articulation, which medical science mediates, situates abortion within cultural practices that harness technology for the control of life and death, but that also channel the substance of expression of life and death into the matter-flows of machinic technologies and processes. On one hand, there is the rationalization of organic matter and biological systems. And on the other hand, there is the rationalization of human bodies as component structures (i.e., as reproducing bodies, or, more recently, reproducing organs) in larger orders, such as ethnic, religious, or classed communities; national labor forces; transnational substitute labor forces and markets (i.e., "third world" sectors); and biomedical economies of consumption and production.

Some aspects of this biomedical assemblage rationalize and commodify the reproduction of the human biomass, through the social reproduction of mothering, for example, or artificial insemination, test-tube fertilization, surrogate mothering, cryostorage of fertilized ova, or cross-uterine egg transplants. Other aspects of the biomedical assemblage channel depredations of the human biomass, as in the case of the AIDS epidemic, for example, in which funding and research protocols guide the epidemic toward specific populations (gay men, inner-city minority women, migrant workers, prisoners). While abortion is an ancient practice that has always existed within the domain of the maternal function, the practice of mass-produced abortion places a politics of depredation in the hands of women, while placing control over the means of production in the hands of the AMA.

Biomedicine, in the substance of expression of legal abortion, both deterritorializes and reterritorializes the gendered social spaces of the feminine. Abortion allows women to control not only their own reproductive processes but also the social function of the maternal; it gives women the ability to choose when and if to be a mother and to better control economic independence. At the same time, abortion facilitates the reterritorialization of the organic maternal by subjecting it to instrumental reason and commodity logic. Abortion enables motherhood to better interface with existing bourgeois social structures of professionalization, careerism, class status, and consumerism, as well as cycles of personal economic prosperity or of national periods of high- or low-growth economics. Abortion in some of its usages both deterritorializes feminine social roles and reterritorializes the human body and its organs of reproduction within the machinic and instrumental logic of late-modern capitalism. For women of different ethnic communities and class investments, the stakes of such adaptations are not equivalent, nor is access to abortion, the costs of it, or the outcomes of it.

The social meaning of abortion practices in the United States has always been a highly contested field of signs. Abortion has raised pragmatic questions regarding who would have control over the local act of reproduction or depredation, in that control of that local act would partially determine demographics within the larger body politic. In the nineteenth century, abortion became more visible as industrial urbanization drew women into the cities and into the workforce. The fertility rate of white American women dropped almost 50 percent from 1800 to 1900, from 7.04 to 3.56 children (Tribe 29). Not surprisingly, this demographic and reproductive shift was accompanied by a nineteenth-century antiabortion movement, with Protestant physicians such as Horatio Storer leading the outcry for criminalization of abortion by 1865. Protestant middle- and upper-class women who were choosing in increasing numbers to interrupt pregnancies were accused of enacting "race suicide," and attention was drawn to the fact that Irish immigrant birthrates were far exceeding native-born Protestant birthrates; in Buffalo in 1855, the former was twice as high as the latter (Tribe 32). Clearly, abortion was seen by these vocal Protestants as eugenic dissipation. Control of abortion in these arguments came to signify eugenic longevity, increased political representation, accumulation of property, and the historical continuity of the group—significations reproduced in contemporary "pro-life" rhetoric. By the turn of the millennium in the United States, women's manifest power over demographic flows, enacted locally as the right to terminate pregnancy, and the struggles of the state and of secular groups to control that power, constituted one of the striking features of becoming-woman at the end of the twentieth century. Whether the act of abortion was called "termination of pregnancy" or "termination of fetal life," at a macro social level, abortion practices were altering the contour and flow of national demographics.

In 1973, the U.S. Supreme Court rendered a decision in *Roe v. Wade* that authorized a woman's individual, naturalized right to bodily autonomy.[2] This right was materialized in social practice as the legalization of unrestricted, elective abortion upon request. The *Roe* ruling set the stage for the mass production and mainstreaming of vacuum-aspiration and vacuum-evacuation abortion technologies and practices in the United States, just as the "baby boomer" generation was reaching its reproductive maturity while rebelling against the familial and reproductive values of their wartime and postwar parents. The number of legal abortions performed per year would double in the decade following 1973, reaching 1.5 million by 1985. This acceleration in the rate of abortions produced a critical point in women's control of reproductive politics. Abortion practices were changing the rate of flow of the biological mass of the U.S. labor force, were changing national as well as ethnic demographics, and were obviously capable of affecting the national standard of living, demands on food supplies and natural resources, military accession rates and recruitment practices, and the stability or instability of future consumer markets. Since abortion practices were now subject to open purview and mediation within the public sphere, the social turbulences surrounding the birth-control practices of women in the United States only intensified after legalization.

Sign-Flow

The power to shape national demographics was obviously never a manifest social right of women, but they gained that social power as an effect of "right to choice." "Choice" became a publicly stated goal of the feminist movement in the United States six years prior to *Roe*, when the "right of women to control their reproductive lives" was added to NOW's Women's Bill of Rights after intense debate at the second national conference of the organization (Tribe 45). Though the feminist counter-use of traditional sex-role ideology inscribed in "motherhood" had helped women peace activists in the early 1960s successfully challenge the House Un-American Activities Committee, NOW decided to risk the public appeal of the maternal image and to put abortion rights on its official agenda. Over the next decade, the feminist counterappropriation of a public voice of maternal morality shifted from antiwar campaigns to antipornography campaigns.

While NOW's leadership and membership struggled over the political and ideological implications of taking up a pro-abortion public platform and image for feminism in the mid-1960s, however, an organized movement to decriminalize abortion in the United States had already emerged from within both the medical and legal professions. The radical feminist notion that unrestricted elective abortion upon request should be every woman's right was popularized in part by a highly mediated medical catastrophe caused by the pharmaceutical industry's irresponsible mass-marketing of thalidomide—an antianxiety drug—to pregnant women.

By 1959, the American Law Institute (ALI) had included in its revised model penal code three defenses to charges of criminal abortion: that continuation of the pregnancy would "gravely impair the physical *or mental health* of the mother"; that the pregnancy was likely to lead to "grave physical or mental defects" in the child; or that the pregnancy resulted from rape or incest (Tribe 36). Two developments in the medical field were reflected in the ALI's new code: an expanded view of health that included psychological and sociological health, and the highly publicized, chemically induced birth defects resulting from the thalidomide scandal starting in the late 1950s. Many practicing physicians saw the thalidomide deformities as appropriate scenarios for eugenic intervention. This view was grounded in the fact that the state of medical technology at the time could have made eugenic feticide in these cases a low-risk and noncomplicated procedure. Many physicians felt in the case of thalidomide-induced birth defects that restrictive state abortion laws were out of touch with medical technologies that made eugenic selection a medical possibility. It would take judicial ruling, however, to transport these technologies into the body politic and transform them into a constitutionally guaranteed individual "right"—the right to a private social space exempt from state jurisdictions applicable to the public sphere. Within that private space, individuals could make decisions without bureaucratic intervention. In 1973, that space was expanded to include the act of abortion. Modern medicine had made removal of the fetus technically possible; juridical ruling made it legal.

In legal terms, abortion was seen as the effect of a private decision. The ruling in *Roe v. Wade* stated that a woman's right to choose an abortion was protected as a constitutional right to individual privacy under the Fourteenth Amendment's "liberty clause" (Tribe 77–112). This remarkable ruling was the result of a confluence of factors, including not only the thalidomide tranquilizer disaster but also an outbreak of rubella from 1962 to 1965, which left some 15,000 babies with birth defects, again raising the issue of eugenic feticide in the popular media (Tribe 37). The juridical precedent in *Roe* came through an analogy between a woman's "right" to terminate a pregnancy and civil rights rulings effected by the Supreme Court's interpretation of a "right to privacy" implied in the Fourteenth Amendment to the Constitution, which guaranteed fundamental "liberty" and due process of law. In *Roe v. Wade*, the Court interpreted this fundamental liberty, with the majority opinion written by Justice Harry Blackmun, as "broad enough to encompass a woman's decision whether or not to terminate her pregnancy" (Tribe 93).

One case precedent for interpreting the Fourteenth Amendment in *Roe v. Wade* to encompass a notion of the right to privacy was the 1967 ruling in *Loving v. Virginia*, which struck down a Virginia law forbidding interracial marriage, thereby adding to the understanding of fundamental rights "the right to choose one's spouse" regardless of race (Tribe 93). The abortion right's debt to the African American civil rights movement went back to the Fourteenth Amendment itself, which, when ratified after the Civil War, constitutionally guaranteed the aims of the 1866 Civil Rights Bill in establishing and protecting African Americans from retaliatory infringement by state legislation in the postwar South.

In 1965, the liberty clause had been successfully invoked against an anticontraception law in Connecticut in order to protect the right of married couples to elect to use contraceptives, and was invoked again in 1972 against a Massachusetts law making contraceptives more difficult for single people to obtain than married people—both rulings implying the fundamental right for individuals "to engage in sexual intercourse without having a child" (Tribe 93–94). In the extension

of the Fourteenth Amendment's liberty clause from issues of race to issues of reproduction, a point of singularity was created that once passed through would generate
a three-decade legacy of social transformation and turbulence. In the leap from legislating the rights of social bodies to act in civil society — to intermingle in marriage
if they so desire, to vote, and so on — to legislating the right to control biological
processes within the interiorities of the human body, the "individual" to whom these
rights belonged became already, clearly, a different kind of subject — one that could
assume technological alterations in biological processes. Both the public sphere and
the space of its private exemptions were being reterritorialized by the state, which
was simultaneously pushing the space of the private and the public inward, into the
interiorities of the human body. Meanwhile, medically engineered reproductive technologies such as the pill were making the material forms of expression of these "fundamental individual rights" conceivable for the first time in history.

      Although the juridical trajectory leading to *Roe v. Wade* had been
laid down in a series of cases tracing back to 1923 in which the Supreme Court evoked
the Fourteenth Amendment against state legislation on the grounds of fundamental
individual rights, this tactic (not characteristic of Western European laws decrimi-
nalizing abortion) would return to haunt the *Roe* decision in the name of the individual rights of the *fetus* (Tribe 74). Meanwhile, the long-standing analogy between
race-based civil rights rulings and gendered ones would be successfully challenged
by a refigured High Court in January 1993 in *Bray v. Alexandria Women's Health Clinic*,
the last abortion ruling rendered during the Bush administration, in which Justice
Scalia wrote the majority opinion (which included Justice Thomas's vote but to which
Justice O'Connor dissented). The ruling rejected an analogy between the Ku Klux
Klan Act and a federal district judge's injunction outlawing abortion clinic blockades
on the grounds that such blockades violated the liberty and due process of women
as a class (Greenhouse). Individual rights discourse began to shift from the rights of
women to the rights of fetuses.

Machinic Propositions

The legalization of abortion as a fundamental, constitutional right of the individual
woman would never have come to pass had it not been for technological advances
in medical practices which rendered abortion a relatively nonproblematic procedure.
Prior to World War II, this was certainly not the case. Death rates from infection
following surgical abortion in New York in the early nineteenth century, even when
performed in hospitals, were over 30 percent, while the mortality rate for childbirth
had dropped to under 3 percent (Tribe 29). One can only speculate at the mortality

rate for women from illegal abortions accomplished by means ranging from poisonous abortifacients to surgical abortion by nonlicensed practitioners. By 1955, the death rate for legal therapeutic abortions was reduced to about one hundred out of every hundred thousand. By 1972, however, one year before *Roe*, the rate had fallen to only three out of every hundred thousand legal therapeutic abortions (Tribe 36).

At the same time that medical sterilization procedures, antibiotics, anesthesia, and vacuum-aspiration technologies (surgical trocars, cannulas, motorized suction) reduced the occurrence of uterine puncture, trauma, hemorrhaging, and postabortion infections, particularly during first-trimester abortion, antibiotics, pesticides, and public health technologies such as water purification and immunization substantially reduced public death rates. Meanwhile, global birthrates continued to rise. Rapid population growth was a striking feature of modernity.

In the two hundred years from 1650 to 1850 the number of people living on earth approximately doubled, from about 500 million to a little over 1 billion. In the one hundred years from 1850 to 1950 the world's population more than doubled again, from about 1 billion to 2.7 billion. Since 1950 the world's population has been increasing at an even faster rate. (Rodman 9)

In general, life seemed to be triumphing over death—with the assistance of human technologies channeling the machinic phylum's self-organizing capabilities in regard to organic and nonorganic matter and energy toward the various physical needs of the "individual" citizen from infancy to old age.

As a result of this biomedical channeling of the machinic phylum, the limit distinguishing life and death became unstable. Currently, for example, "death" has become a question of the point at which life-support technologies that simulate bodily organ-functions should not be continued, while on the other end of the spectrum the beginning of "life" has undergone redefinition in relation to the capabilities of technologies to track, register, and represent intelligible "signs" of its presence, or to extend medical "viability" (the ability to live outside the mother's womb) to younger and younger fetuses. The legal definition of the beginning of fetal life in the early nineteenth century was "quickening"—the point at which the mother could register the fetus's movement in the womb, and the first statutory abortion law in the United States, established in 1821, criminalized termination of pregnancy only *after* quickening (Tribe 29). Within two decades, however, the medical standardization of scientific method in regard to human embryology led many doctors to abandon the quick and nonquick distinction (Tribe 31). Abortion, unregulated in this country until 1821 (meaning it was informally supervised by women), was taken under the jurisdiction of two masculine disciplines—medicine and the law. In the process, the contradictions produced by the subject-object reifications of the medical discipline when juxtaposed with the reifications of the "individual" subject-citizen of jurisprudence and *her rights* would generate several forms of social turbulence.

By the mid-nineteenth century, the American Medical Association (AMA) had launched a lobby to criminalize abortion, not in order to eliminate abortion, but to bring it within the domain of professionalized medicine. Criminalization would allow the AMA to police its professional borders against medical irregulars, midwives, and apothecaries (Tribe 30). From the mid- to late nineteenth century, abortion laws abandoned the distinction between quick and nonquick fetuses, criminalizing all abortion except for "therapeutic" abortion when judged necessary by the physician to save the pregnant woman's life (Tribe 34). Legal therapeutic abortion thus became a matter of the "medical judgment" of the attending physician, and remained so until *Roe v. Wade* in 1973. Ironically, it was the American Medical Association's lobby *for* decriminalization of abortion that helped overturn this long-standing practice.

The threshold for change in the AMA's attitude toward legal abortion was both technical and pragmatic—the relative safety for women of scientifically standardized abortion procedures, particularly during the first and early second trimester, compared to the increasing hazard of legal liability for doctors who in practice interpreted the "therapeutic" clauses liberally. Doctors were not the only ones policing their professional borders; as fewer women died from abortion procedures in the 1950s, decisions to abort for so-called therapeutic reasons came under more scrutiny from formalized hospital review boards, so that the number of legal abortions decreased even as abortion procedures became safer. Doctors who had been liberal in their interpretations of the law in practice needed more license in order to protect their professional judgments in abortion cases from litigation (Tribe 36). In 1970, the AMA pushed for legislatures to codify medical abortion practices, issuing a public statement favoring the legalization of all abortion, limited only by the doctor's own clinical judgment—a complete reversal of its public policy one century earlier but with the same political goal of publicly protecting its professional borders. By now its professional territories were threatened more by the American Bar Association than by unlicensed practitioners (Tribe 38).

The dramatic drop in mortality rates for abortion in the United States was the result of the AMA's professionalization and standardization of medical procedures for surgical abortion. The standardization of vacuum-aspiration abortion was an important factor in decreasing medical complications. That standardization, however, already reified a commodification and technologization of the machinic phylum, in that the procedure was dependent upon development of motorized aspirators, vacurette and vacuum-curettage technologies, and their mass production by the medical supply industry. Motorized vacuum extraction of the fetus, up until the sixteenth week, remains the recommended procedure in the United States, whereas in Japan, where abortion has been legal and effectively available upon request since 1949, irritation of the pregnant uterus by inserting into the cervix a laminaria stick (compressed and sterilized kelp) is common practice, with medical journals reporting no serious complications from this nonmachinic procedure when accompanied with preventative antibiotics (Rodman 56, Tribe 60). The use of laminaria was once fairly common in the United States among pregnant women and abortionists, but was represented as highly dangerous by the AMA during the nineteenth-century movement toward criminalization of non-medically supervised abortion. Only recently have some U.S. doctors begun to reconsider laminaria techniques as a safe and nontraumatic method for legal abortion. Properly placed, laminaria absorb cervical secretions, cause painless dilation of the cervix, stimulate uterine contraction, and result in miscarriage within a few days (Rodman 63). In the United States, however, surgical feticide was big business. By the early 1970s, AMA-controlled, mechanized abortion had begun to function as a sign for women's parity in the labor market. By 1970, 43 percent of working-age women were in the labor force, with the percentage of white married women working outside the home doubling in the two decades between 1950 and 1970 (Tribe 39). Women were being fully integrated in the workplace, the professions, and higher education. The fertility rate among women in the United States dropped from 3.7 in the mid-1950s to 1.8 in 1975. Fertility control, including contraception in the case of the pill, feticide in cases of surgical abortion, and prevention of zygote implantation with intrauterine devices (IUDs) allowed not only upper-class women but also women in a burgeoning middle class to choose to delay either marriage or childbearing or both, or simply to choose not. For each class, fertility control could threaten existing power relations in a different way. Fertility control in upper-class women could alter the intergenerational accumulation of property as well as political representation at the polls. Reproductive rates of middle-class women could affect the future consuming class, determining the stability of future marketing sectors, while working-class fertility control could affect manpower supplies and shortages for the next generation's laboring class—including laboring bodies for military accession. Obviously, class differences correlate to racial differentials as well. Recall, for example, that by 1992, black women made up 48.7 percent of all women in the army's enlisted ranks, as black men and women were driven in inordinate numbers into military service by poor opportunities in the civilian business sector.

While most research suggests that abortion rates did not actually rise after legalization, the formerly onerous status of abortion did change. There were also fewer class restrictions on privileged access to safe abortion and standardization of safer medical procedures. While the number of abortions rose as the population increased with the sexual maturity of the "baby boomer" generation, the percentage of abortions remained fairly stable before and after legalization; however, fewer women died from the procedure or experienced complications after legalization, and women in general felt less compulsion to hide the fact that they had had an abortion (Ide, Rodman, Tribe). By 1973, the practice of abortion had gone public, it had become mechanized, and it was bureaucratically supervised by the AMA. And for four years until the first Hyde Amendment annulled Medicaid abortion in 1977, women from all classes had access to safe abortion (Faludi, Snitow).

These changes in the practice of abortion are only one aspect of a larger scene of political contention and transmogrification arising around the capacities of new medical technologies to alter human biological processes of reproduction and death. Control over birth-control technologies, including vacuum-aspiration abortion before seven weeks since Last Menstrual Period (also known as dilation and evacuation, or D&E, from eight to sixteen weeks); antiprogestins such as RU 486 (a menstrual "inductor" that works by interfering with the action of progesterone, preventing a fertilized ovum from implanting in the uterine wall); and applications of new reproductive technologies such as tissue farming, test-tube fertilization, and cross-uterine egg transplants, lie at the core of a growing social turbulence over the future of what is manifestly a human-machinic reorganization of the body politic.

In this regard, FDA approval and commercial distribution in the United States of antiprogestins such as RU 486 have become NOW's high priority in the current social debate over abortion legislation. Such technologically engineered compounds will make many of the specific issues in the current legal battle over abortion moot and post-*Webster* pro-choice political strategies outdated, such as state-to-state legal battles and media campaigns against each newly instituted state law restricting abortion, with contested state legislation going to a conservatively restructured anti-*Roe* Supreme Court majority. That majority, ameliorated by President Clinton's appointment of Justice Ruth Bader Ginsberg in the summer of 1993, was demonstrated in the 1989 ruling on *William Webster v. Reproductive Health Services* when the High Court upheld a Missouri law requiring the attending physician to test for "fetal viability" on any woman whom he or she believed to be twenty or more weeks pregnant, in spite of the fact that current medical practice does not recommend amnio-centesis—the only available procedure for testing fetal lung viability—until twenty-eight to thirty weeks of gestation due to health risks to the pregnant woman and the fetus (Tribe 21). In this regard, the *Webster* ruling gestured a return to the statutory distinction between quick and unquick fetuses established in 1821, with the concept undergoing technological transformation into "fetal viability," and with the status of "viability" (both as a fetal state and as a measurement of that state) manifestly subject to machinic advances in medical technologies. Needless to say, the regulatory mechanism of the *Webster* ruling works by placing the attending physician's judgment under public review with the threat of liability if a review board disagrees with the physician's judgment in any given case.

With RU 486, however, which causes shedding of the embryo after implantation in the uterine wall, abortion can be self-administered for seven weeks from the Last Menstrual Period (Tribe 214–15). Because of the form of expression such antiprogestins render to abortion, they could never be policed in the way that licensed physicians performing surgical abortions can be; they transform a surgical procedure into a pill that can be self-administered. Regulation and policing would therefore have to take place through bureaucratic regulation of distribution. From the point of view of technology, antiprogestins at least potentially can remove abortion from the public sphere and place it within the private sphere of the individual woman—while de facto constituting that private space as such. Likewise, the public judgment of the doctor required in *Webster* could be transformed into the private decision of the pregnant woman. With RU 486, both the doctor and the clinic/hospital—the sites of current regulatory policing—could virtually disappear from the initial stage of the abortion. Indeed, antiprogestins mark a potential point of singularity in regard to technology in which what we have come to know as "abortion" (rationalized as mass-produced vacuum-aspirator machines) can potentially undergo a transformation to "menstrual induction."

The lobby to regulate abortion practices by making access and funding more difficult and time consuming, and liability greater for doctors performing abortions, accelerated in the 1980s, even as research and development directed toward channeling the machinic phylum into eugenic, biogenetic, and artificial reproduction technologies boomed. The simplicity, safety, and self-administering quality of antiprogestins such as RU 486, currently still unapproved for use in this country though the U.S. Academy of Sciences ruled in September 1993 that the FDA should expedite its evaluation for U.S. marketing, present the most immediate challenge to this counterwave, or to use Faludi's (1991) preferred term, *backlash* against a woman's (at least at one time) naturalized (constitutional) right to bodily autonomy (i.e., to choose whether or not to be a mother, to choose to have sex without being a parent, to choose not to carry a pregnancy to term, to choose to regulate fetal life and death, to choose to abort one's fetus). While the lobby against *Roe* was producing antiabortion judicial appointments in the federal courts and Supreme Court throughout the 1980s and early 1990s until President Clinton's pro-choice appointment of Justice Ginsberg, research and development investment monies were flowing into the fertility and surrogate motherhood industries. The idea of artificial wombs had become a historical fact by the time *Webster* provided a politically realigned Supreme Court the opportunity in 1989 to challenge a woman's constitutional right to unrestricted abortion upon request in the first two trimesters.

Technologically, the steroid compound RU 486 or any comparable antiprogestin compound constitutes a threshold that, once passed through, will inevitably alter the terms of the current social debate and the concept of abortion as we have known it. Successful political organization supporting legalization of antiprogestins could in effect make many of the High Court's current battles over state regulation of abortion ineffectual. Antiabortion coalitions would be forced to assert that life begins at conception—an argument that is more overtly religious than scientific—while losing their most powerful popular icon (the aborted developed second-trimester fetus), as technology would in this case shift the debate from the rights of fetuses to the rights of zygotes and fertilized ova, which at the time of early termination with RU 486 cannot always be technically distinguished from the cells of tumors and menstrual tissue.

Politically, the organized lobby to legalize antiprogestins might also have to overcome a structural resistance from the now well-established political economy of the medical industry, from medical equipment manufacturers and distributors who produce vacuum aspirators, to the clinics and doctors who specialize in abortion services. The popular dissemination of antiprogestins and knowledge about how to self-administer them properly would in effect put the extensive development of these portions of the medical industry into an almost immediate supply surplus, although some of those same clinics and professionals would logically be an appropriate network for administering health care to women using antiprogestins that require a hormonal injection two days after ingestion to increase the effectivity of the compound. Current research shows that RU 486, when taken within seven weeks LMP and when combined within forty-eight hours with an injection of the hormone prostaglandin, which causes uterine contractions, was 95 percent to 100 percent effective in causing uterine shedding of the fertilized embryo (i.e., inducing menstruation)

(Tribe 214, Rodman 54). It may be later determined that the prostaglandin injection could also be technologically transformed into a self-administered form, although now that injection serves nicely as a trafficking mechanism guiding users through the clinical apparatus.

Within an economy of repetition, the mechanism for bureaucratic control over artificially manufactured abortifacient compounds (natural abortifacient plants having successfully been policed out of common use by the AMA by the mid-nineteenth century) will be through networks of distribution, which is why U.S. pro-life coalitions threatened boycott of French developer Groupe Roussel Uclaf's U.S. subsidiary (Tribe 216). Until Clinton's inauguration, the strategy had worked, though even without Clinton's timely repeal of Republican edicts on abortion, including the ban on abortion counseling in federally financed clinics and a review of the ban on RU 486, it would have been only a matter of time before an economy of proliferation would have caused the antiabortion coalition's bureaucratic control to disintegrate. As happened with the pill, some small company with little to lose and much to gain could request permission from the FDA to market a variation of antiprogestin for other medical purposes (research suggests usefulness in treatments for endometriosis and breast cancer), at which point a consumer economy would take over. The social relations regulating feticide at that point will have undergone an incorporeal transformation from the doctor-patient to pharmacist-consumer relationship—the latter then becoming the site for future bureaucratic and legislative regulation. As it stands now, Clinton's policy change on RU 486 has opened the door for even large pharmaceutical manufacturers to move toward developing and distributing antiprogestins in the United States.

RU 486 will not, however, change the structural reification of social relations inscribed in the biomedical channeling of reproductive technologies. The hard fact is that the cultural construction of a woman's right to "choice" in *Roe v. Wade* (that is, her naturalized right to bodily autonomy) is a reification, by objectification of the child, of the social relations of mothers and children into *individual subjects* and *fetus-objects*, just as much as pro-life rhetoric and artificial and substitute womb industries reify the maternal-child relation into *fetus subjects* and *womb-objects*. In this regard, pro-life rhetoric is actually astute in its insistence that abortion is a reification of feticide. This realization, however, has not led pro-life coalitions to address the contradiction in their politics and rhetoric of opposing abortion in a culture that does not have a systematic policy for reproductive education in its public schools, that has an outrageously high teenage pregnancy rate, and that fails to provide adequate child services.[3] Such rhetoric denies the fact that motherhood against one's choosing (i.e., motherhood in poverty, physical hardship, or excessively large families, motherhood in youth or old age, motherhood in depression, in emotionally or physically abusive relationships, in dysfunctional families, or after rape or incest constitutes a socially condoned violence against women and their children.

The pro-life analysis stops before the imminent conclusion of its own logic — that our everyday social relations *are* violent, that in fact all of our social relations bear *degrees* of violence. This realization is precisely what it desires to disavow, by projecting onto abortion and the women who choose to abort the status of a heinous act. Barbara Johnson's reading of abortion reminds us of this regrettable yet commonplace fact. The "choice" of abortion puts women in the conflicted situation of being both subjects and objects of violence at the same time — choosing not between violence or nonviolence, but between violences, between kinds of violence, "between simple violence to a fetus and complex, less determinate violence to an involuntary mother and/or an unwanted child" (Johnson 191).

The irony is that the very logic that empowered individual women to "evacuate uterine contents" also empowers (fetal) individuals with the right to live in womb-objects, either the womb-objects in which they were conceived, or in artificial or surrogate womb-objects. This is the same rationalization of individual rights that reifies the subjection of third-world labor to poverty and third-world populations to death-by-exposure in order for first-world "individuals" to maintain an inordinately high standard of living. It is the same logic that rationalizes the practice of amniocentesis followed by female-specific feticide in some Asian countries (a technological variation on the long-standing practice of female infanticide), even as international electronics economies and garment industries depend upon the cheap labor of Asian working girls. And it is the same logic that not so long ago denied women social agency in other than reproductive and domestic terms. In the historical moment of unveiling to public purview this once well-guarded secret that women can carry out depredatory functions even as mothers, women need more than ever to articulate for themselves an ethics and politics of depredation. The articulation of such an ethics and politics might very well begin with those very depredations that have allowed the subjects of late-capitalist feminisms to come into historical being as such. These systematic depredations, material yet often unrepresentable (compare the number of mainstream films in which a woman decides to have an abortion to the commonplaceness of abortion in the United States), mark the flows of power crossing feminine social bodies, and their artificial substitutes, in postmodernity. And as they generate turbulence in the balance of social power between women and the state, they also provide the psychic fuel feeding projected and obsessive cultural nightmares about female predations.

F   I   V   E

Lesbians and the
Serial Killing-Machine

Lizzie Borden took an ax

And gave her father forty whacks.

When she saw what she had done,

She gave her mother forty-one.

In an epoch marked by mass-produced feticide and a militarized feminine, it's not surprising that the cinematic screen-machine is projecting a symptomatic nightmare image for public consumption: the woman who murders more than once, in cold blood. The semic code organizing this cultural figure is hardly new, however. The myth of Lizzie Borden provided a prototype of the contemporary feminine predator emerging within the popular-image repertoire of late nineteenth-century America. While in actuality Borden was acquitted of murder charges (the case hinged upon the prosecution's inability to find the murder weapon and the appeal of prominent members of the community on Borden's behalf), the Borden myth both popularized the threat of a feminine-predatory subject and contained it within the rubric of familial crimes of hate (i.e., patricide and matricide) or within the rubric of an asystematic psychotic break within the individual (i.e., insanity).

While the Borden myth reminds us that the feminine predator is not a new figure in U.S. popular culture, it also highlights the signifying difference in 1990s iterations of this old trope of dangerous femininity—that difference being the association of the feminine predator with a manifest homoeroticism. It's my premise here, however, that the new queer mark on this old predatory body screens a repetition that is in actuality the more telling signifier in this story of social violence and gendered identity—a repetition that points us toward a contagion of social violences so vast that it is threatening, as it is always threatening, to exceed the constative rationalizations of our notion of abstract justice. This excess of justice, which is the same as saying justice's failure, in regard to the lesbian's public faciality symptomatizes a failure to reify as "just" what is blatantly a sacrificial exchange of social bodies and social violences in which the lesbian channels violence for the community. I want to return for a moment more to the history of this screen projection whose being has been being sent, both to the lesbian "I" and to the other, for the long duration of a tumultuous and violent century.

The mass production of the myth of a female predator was delivered into the twentieth century by the technology and broadcast distribution of the popular fiction industry and later the cinema. By the 1920s, 1930s, and 1940s, the hard-boiled detective stories and crime novels of the Hammett/Chandler/Spillane tradition had modernized and Americanized the genre of crime fiction made immensely popular by Sir Arthur Conan Doyle in the Sherlock Holmes series, which spanned the turn of the century from the 1880s to the 1920s. One of Dashiell Hammett's trademark innovations on Doyle's classic formula in his Continental Op stories, published in the 1920s and 1930s, was the insertion into the narrative of a type of murderous female character whose capacity to kill precisely exceeded the discursive limits of familial hate crimes. That her predations, rendered in classics such as "The Girl with the Silver Eyes," exceeded those of familial crimes of hate, however, only suggested all the more that her figure, like Borden's, was signifying symptomatically the breakdowns of a dysfunctioning nuclear family. Raymond Chandler in the 1930s and 1940s continued to develop this murderous feminine character type, placing her in a social landscape of crime and violence in which moral conclusions were rarely drawn and in which truth and justice were manifestly determined by money and power, epitomized in his first novel *The Big Sleep* (1939). In the American milieu of signs in which the wealth, status, and tradition of Sir Arthur Conan Doyle's social order were overturned by greed, economic inequities, organized crime, and everyday immorality, the dark woman of crime fiction was becoming unanchored from both the protection and morality of the domestic sphere. In the fiction of Mickey Spillane, the detective's aggressivity toward the dark lady of crime was becoming overtly murderous and violent. In *I the Jury* (1947), for example, the detective Mike Hammer realizes that the woman he has been erotically desiring is also the criminal he is pursuing. Rather than arresting her in the tradition of Hammett's Sam Spade, however, he empties his revolver into her crotch.

Throughout the 1930s and 1940s, this figure of a female predator was further popularized for broadcast audiences in the immensely successful genre of film noir, where she reigned supreme on the cinema's ghostly projection screen as the deadly yet seductive femme fatale. Reproducing the destabilization of gendered signs and identities that this figure of dangerous femininity introduced into crime fiction, she typically appeared in classic noir at center screen only to become by film's end either the arrested body that would rationalize the police force (as in Roy Del Ruth's and John Huston's filmic versions of Hammett's *The Maltese Falcon* [1931, 1941]), or the reassimilated wife rationalizing patrilineal property rights and validating the marriage system as signifier of a healthy social body (as in Michael Curtiz's *Casablanca* [1942]).

In the late 1950s and 1960s, television's electronic medium would conduct the spectre of this feminine predator, assimilating noir's claustrophobic mise-en-scène to the TV studio, and freeing the cinematic apparatus to produce a technologically innovative product in the 1960s less suitable to televisual mimesis and appropriation. This new product was the panoramic, cinemascopic Western—a nostalgic projection monumental enough to screen the translocation of the U.S. frontier from North America to Southeast Asia. Meanwhile, the collapse of the Hollywood studio system in the 1960s, assisted by TV's competition, pushed the filmic detective genre toward further disintegration as a containment mechanism for the very phantom projection it had mass-produced.

By 1974, the channeling of violence through the fatal woman's phantom projection virtually imploded on the silver screen in Polanski's *Chinatown*, a film in which the femme fatale is an incest victim who, though innocent of any crime, is shot in the eye at film's end by the police, while the evil father makes off with his daughter/granddaughter wrapped in his incestuous arms as she screams hysterically for her dead mommy. Against this historical backdrop of imprisoned and dead femmes fatales, transformations in 1990s popular representations of women-who-kill appear not as a rupture or discontinuity, but as qualitative changes in the woman's relation to the predatory act, to the tools of violence and organs of predation, and to the ability of the modern legal system to successfully screen either feminine depredations or the constative production of women as sacrificial victims of social violence.

In addition, the new movie genre coined by *Mirabella*'s June 1992 issue as "psychofemme" films—a genre that includes *Thelma and Louise*, *Single White Female*, and *Basic Instinct*, among many others—increasingly depicts a failure of the heterosexual economy to regulate and contain homoerotic exchanges between women.

In 1974, the popular narrative in *Chinatown* screened by Hollywood to a post-civil rights, post-Watergate, and post-Vietnam public depicted the police and a patrilineal property system as the embodiments of, not the protections against, a systematic violence toward women. Nearly twenty years later, the 1990s cinema has been busily (dis)organizing a cultural representation of an angry and vengeful woman—a woman who threatens to step beyond the bounds of heterosexual exchange—into two screen bodies, two clichéd images, which are two faces of the same fatal figure whose cold-blooded depredations threaten the nuclear family, the state police force, and heterosexual law and order. One of those screen bodies channels violence toward men and the nuclear family while escaping not only the economies of clan retribution and sacrificial substitution that the modern justice system supposedly displaced, but also the modern justice system itself. This screen woman is embodied paradigmatically in Sharon Stone's unpunished predations in *Basic Instinct* in 1992. Her body double, in contradistinction, channels violence toward men and the nuclear family, but is in turn subject to both a narrative economy of violent retribution and a symbolic economy within the public sphere of ritual sacrifice. The fate of the double is epitomized by Madonna's bloody, sacrificial expenditure at the end of *Body of Evidence*, which appeared one year after *Basic Instinct*'s release.

Similarly, if *Basic Instinct* depicts a lesbian predator who kills yet eludes both retribution and justice, it's because her lesbian double in the film, Roxy, dies in her place, while Catherine Tremell succumbs to a heterosexual exchange from a homosexual plenitude. In spite of that exchange, however tentative if not volatile it is rendered by the film's doubled ending, the predatory screen face projected in *Basic Instinct* does not reassimilate into the nuclear family, nor does she become the target of violent retribution. And in a now common deviation from classic noir narratives, she also does not go to jail, eluding reappropriation and containment under a modern economy of abstract justice embodied by the state police and juridical system. It's hardly coincidental that this juridical system was revealed in the streets of Los Angeles, in the same year as *Basic Instinct*'s release, to be no more than a veil for violent retribution and overt racism, and it was exposed as such by the unofficial video documenting Rodney King's beating at the hands of L.A. police, which came to haunt the U.S. court system as well as the evening news.

It's not surprising, then, that the danger represented by Stone's predations, only tentatively contained by her marginally secured heterosexuality, is transducted into violence toward her body double, a woman who kills men and is violently killed by them in turn, embodying an exchange of violences not rationalized by a system of abstract justice as in classic noir, but by vengeful retribution on the level of the individual narrative and by sacrificial substitution on the level of an intertextual public sphere. In other words, if Sharon Stone can walk after both lesbianism and serial murder in *Basic Instinct*, a sacrificial screen body no less culturally loaded than a post-*Sex*, bisexual Madonna must be offered up for a mass act of ritual murder, partly played in slow motion with background music, in *Body of Evidence*'s normalizing repetition of *Instinct*'s aberrations against the legitimate exchange of social bodies and social violences. The most symptomatic difference, then, in 1990s screenings of this old threat of feminine violence lies in the now doubled representation of the law's inability to regulate either the social violence channeled toward this woman or the violence that she channels toward the socius. Both bodies expose a system of violent exchanges once screened by the communally held and officially sanctioned pretense of an abstract and therefore just equivalency under the law. Whether the woman walks after lesbianism and serial murder or whether she is blown away in an unveiled spasm of violent retribution in the spirit of *Fatal Attraction*'s (1987) vulgar, public bloodletting, 1990s filmic representations of feminine predators figure a woman who is beyond both the punishment *and* protection of the justice system and its police force — beyond precisely that which was challenged but always finally rationalized and legitimized in classic noir.

Obviously, the lesbian and gay community needs to do just violence to this screen projection of a lesbian psychofemme predator, but in doing so, it also needs to address the broader and more difficult issue of the proper collective relation to a contagion of social violences. That is, the nightmare projection of a lesbian predator directs us to take up the more general question of how to represent, to ourselves and to the other, violence's past and the past of violence in the lesbian community. Because beyond that question, an even more pressing issue faces us — the issue of violences and resistances in our own discourses about collective identities and public representations. Taking this broad approach to the relation of lesbians and social violence within the general economy will require several detours that we will later find are only rerouting opportunities for the essential adestination of lesbian identities who have sent their being and who have had their being sent into the collision course of becoming-woman and becoming killing-machine.

In the first week of January 1993, the *New York Times* reported that AIDS had become the leading cause of death in the New York State prison system, while the U.S. military had renewed "low intensity" bombing raids in Iraq to stabilize "global security." Later that same month, the Joint Chiefs of Staff announced to the public their resistance to Clinton's campaign promise to end the 1948 ban of gay men and lesbians in the military, citing the violent beating-murder of a gay sailor by his mates as an example of the "disciplinary" problems that could arise from revoking the ban. By the end of January, three marines in Wilmington, North Carolina, pulled a patron out of a gay bar and fractured his skull, shouting "Clinton must pay" (*New York Times*, February 2, 1993). The following week in the Bronx, a young African American man suffering from seizures and a drug problem, who had been in and out of shelters, prisons, and emergency rooms for years, beat an eighty-year-old woman to death with a lead pipe outside her church (*New York Times*, February 7, 1993). Five months earlier in Cleveland, a lesbian had murdered her lover, saying that the lover's father had harassed his daughter for being a lesbian to the point that she announced, "I wish I was dead" (Pontoni). In his study of the systematization of violence in the *The Nervous System* (1992), Mick Taussig recounts the story of a woman who, when approached by a social worker who has arrived to take her last remaining child as a ward of the state, pulls down her pants and reveals a stab wound in her butt. Upon realizing what she'd done, she pulls up her pants and laughs nervously.

What I'm suggesting is that we live in an epoch of continuous violences, and in this our epoch differs little from previous ones, except perhaps that today the right to participate in military predatory systems has come to signify the full social status and civil rights of the individual citizen, whether that citizen be lesbian or gay, a woman, or African American. It's from this epochal perspective of the general economy that I seek the proper affect with which to approach the lesbian body that Sharon Stone's projection in *Basic Instinct* screens as body double. That body, which could never appear unscreened in the public sphere, belongs to Aileen Wuornos, who, one year before *Basic Instinct*'s release, was arrested for murdering seven men on seven separate occasions along a rural highway in south Florida, and who was labeled by the media as "the first lesbian serial killer."

Bearing Wuornos's body and public sign in mind, I want you to recall the mediated outrage from the lesbian and gay community, vocalized by Queer Nation, Out in Film, and the national Gay and Lesbian Alliance Against Defamation (GLAAD), in regard to *Basic Instinct*'s 1992 portrayal of the lesbian as serial killer (*New York Times*, March 29, 1992). We all know that gays and lesbians as liminal and marginalized social bodies are particularly susceptible to the channeling of social violence, as are other minority bodies. The proportion of *psychofemme* lesbians to appear on the silver screen compared to the total number of lesbians in general to appear on-screen speaks for itself as to the state of just and equivalent representation in the mainstream cinema, and epitomizes the use of the lesbian body to channel and then screen a potential contagion of violence erupting from the breakdown of the sex-gender system in the so-called "healthy" heterosexual social body. But in order to understand the systematicity of violence within the killing-machine—what Taussig (1992) terms "terror as usual" in the Nervous System—and in order to understand the roles that lesbian bodies play within such a system, we must go further than the just and timely protests by Glaad, Queer Nation, and Out in Film, and be willing to push on to question the politics of violence and resistance in the stories we tell *about* violence in the lesbian community as well as in the mainstream media, both in the official and unofficial representations of violence and in our personal and public representations of violence (38).

For a few moments, then, I want to pretend we don't have to tell this official and utopic story anymore in which lesbians, like U.S. citizens in general, and like women in general, are nonviolent social subjects, in an argument that attempts to protect lesbians from the violence of social defamation (and the physical and emotional brutality that goes with it) by claiming their own innocence from participation in violent systems of social exchange. This claim touches us all the more painfully when we allow ourselves to know what is everywhere obvious, that all systems of social exchange known to men and women in our culture depend upon systematic exchanges of violence. Some of those violences are sacred, legitimate, and public; others are criminal, illegitimate, and covert. And the regulation and breakdown of that distinction is precisely the domain of the killing-machine.

Let's make no mistake that the unifying factor in the disparate group of "legitimate" victims of violence is their liminal status on the fringes of society—the degree of their dis-integration within the legitimating discourses of the healthy socius (Girard). Because of their marginalized status, the exposure of these social bodies to violence entails little risk of reprisal from any empowered social group. The constative exchange structuring the sacrifice is thus an act of violence without risk of vengeance. It's within this economy of exchanges, which the modern justice system supposedly replaced, that we can begin to understand the meaning of the lesbian serial killer's serialized and mediated signature. Once protected from sacrificial substitution because of risk of clan retaliation, women become subject to increasing social violence with the breakdown first of local communities and later of the nuclear family. As the social link between women and the larger community disintegrates, women, particularly single women or women outside of the economy of heterosexual exchange, become increasingly marked for violence. The serial killing-machine typically preys on women who were once protected by the status of the local clan as it was reproduced in women's maternal function. Thus, single women are particularly susceptible to serial killing, as exemplified by the Green River slayings of prostitutes in Washington State, Ted Bundy's interstate murder spree of young single white women, and the Gainesville murders of white coeds at the University of Florida. Deterritorializing local cultural geographies of class and race in order to reterritorialize them under a regime of terror, the serial killer is typically itinerant, often using transportation technologies to better prey on the disintegrating social ties of broken-down communities in which neighbors don't visually recognize or speak to neighbors and the comings and goings of "strangers" can no longer be policed by communal social bonds.

In the late modern cinema's projection of a lesbian predator, the failure of the clan system to regulate social violence toward women takes a new turn. In *Single White Female* (1992), the murders are committed specifically to spite the clan, as well as the feminine positions of "het" daughter and wife that the kinship system authorizes. In *Basic Instinct*, the murders are against the clan. If nothing else, *Basic Instinct* projects the breakdown of the nuclear family system: mothers who kill their children, daughters who kill their parents, girlfriends who murder lovers, girlfriends who are lesbians, female psychotherapists who hate their male patients, women who hate the idea of domesticity and childrearing, phallic women who expose gaps in the law, femmes fatales who murder the detective. This projected nightmare drives the fantasmatic narrative to its nearly classic resolution—the detective murders the murderous lesbian double, becomes the object of the femme fatale's desire, and reestablishes phallic order (...almost).

In the case of Wuornos, the murders are both against the clan and in and of themselves the revenge of the clan, which she has taken upon herself to execute—that is, they stand in the place of an absent clan revenge while they also stand in judgment against domestic violence within the clan. In court testimony, Wuornos maintained that she killed only those johns who "deserved it." Aileen Wuornos, as a homeless lesbian highway prostitute, is the liminal body that should have constituted the body of the sacrificial victim. Refusing that role, she chooses instead, illegitimately, the position of the sacrificial priest, the judge, and the executioner—until she is caught by the police and brought under the judication of the legal system, where the power of the act of violence that she deterritorialized for her own signature is reterritorialized by the Law and redirected toward Wuornos as a proper body for social violence in the form of the death sentence.

Serial killing treads the liminal social space between sacrifice and murder—between the impure sacred and the criminal. It is a form of anonymous violence that foils retribution from a community, becoming then a game of outwitting the state police force. It exists in the space between the emptied function of the local community and family clan in the late modern state and the state and national judicial system. Its intercounty or interstate flight is countered only by an intrastate and interstate police data system. In this sense, serial killing is a game played with an abstract-machine (deductive rational logic authorized as the law and institutionalized as a computerized police surveillance and data-processing system) in which the serial killer tracks the disintegrating or missing social links through which the body politic reproduces and rationalizes power, rather than an exchange executed through a body within the context of a specific community.

In an economy of sacrifice, the desire to commit acts of violence toward those near us is channeled to bodies on the margins of society, thereby quelling a potential contagion of violences within the legitimate socius. Serial killing spurs rather than quells a contagion of violence the more it takes inappropriate and illegitimate victims as its target—white coeds as the privileged daughters of the rising bourgeois middle class or nouveau riche in the case of the Gainesville murders, for example, or, in the case of Wuornos, white heterosexual men. It's not surprising that this contagion of violence is then redirected toward "appropriate" victims, just as south Florida newspapers reported that hate crimes against lesbians increased during the period of Wuornos's trial (Brownworth).

The machinically assembled "seriature" of the lesbian serial killer—a term coined by Ronell in her reading of Rodney King's assembled media representation in *Haunted TV* (1992)—is the effect of a network of media representations. This network constituting Wuornos's public signature as serial killer—her seriature—includes Hollywood projections of women who kill and media coverage of Wuornos as the "first lesbian serial killer" in the form of news reports, coverage of the trial on *Court TV,* and the made-for-TV movie *Overkill.* This network produces mediating windows through which the socius polices itself through the perpetual threat of pandemonium from an imaginary exterior. The temporal flow of rational consciousness in TV then frames, formats, and fractures this pandemonium that it constitutes. In the process, the face of the serial killer can only sign in the public sphere as manifestly posthuman, in that it signs as the concrete form of expression of an abstract machine mediating social violences. In this mediation, which now constitutes the public sphere, the post-Cartesian body signs as "I am because I appear on network news."

In the made-for-TV movie depicting the Wuornos story, for example, television simulated its own call to ethics as realistic docudrama. That which was usually hidden from view suddenly burst in mimetic packaging replete with interrupting commercials onto the broadcast screen of evening TV—as the ugly scene of social violence embodied in the "robbing" of a street prostitute (i.e., rape) and even more censored because far more violently contagious for the community—*the revenge of the robbed prostitute* who is both a lesbian and an incest "survivor." *Overkill* signifies first and foremost revenge rather than self-defense. Aileen Wuornos as "seriated" killer serialized by her mediated signature is the liminal scapegoat who refuses to become the sacrificial body she is marked to be by channeling social violence rather than absorbing it, by refusing to eat the poisonous *pharmakon* (first as the phallus and penis of the incestuous grandfather and uncle, later as the hard-on of the abusive and robbing trick) by which she would be transformed into the sacrificial body as lower-class, lesbian, second-generation incest victim and streetwalker whose tricks often enough don't even pay her (i.e., in street slang they "rob" her). Instead of eating this poison of the socius, she *becomes* the poison that must in turn be eaten by the sick community in a blatantly sacrificial exchange reified as an economy of abstract justice, in order for that economy and that community to be cured of the outcomes of its own violence—that is, in order to represent to itself the normative "health" of its everyday social relations. This is the circuit of mediated exchanges into which Aileen Wuornos sends her identity and has her identity sent as lesbian serial killer.

Wuornos's violence is the effect and the affect of an illegitimate social identity that can only become legitimate as serial killer. In Eve Sedgwick's terms laid out in an article on queer performativity (1993), the extent to which Wuornos doesn't have a legitimate identity is the extent to which she has an identity of shame. Her performance of her shame, and shamelessness, is the only way she has to legitimate—that is, to make visible and intelligible to herself and to the other—the affect of anger, which constitutes her identity as one who is unable to *be* as legitimate identity, but who refuses either to annihilate herself through suicide or to be the murdered body in the woods.

Her seriature is reterritorialized, assembled, and regulated by an interstate police, computer database, broadcast media network. Even as she threatens the legitimacy of that network, she evokes the "justified" use of police force, thereby providing the body upon which the social system's unjust violences can be reified as abstract justice. She both threatens to rupture the illusion of nonviolent social relations within the body politic and provides the individuated body through which the body politic can represent itself as nonviolent and just. Her telemediated identity is framed and serialized just as her telemediated trial was being serialized on *Court TV.* For the television viewer of *Overkill* (which received vociferous mail complaining that Wuornos was represented too sympathetically), there is an uncanny recognition of the familiar in Wuornos's bizarre docudrama—her life *is* docudrama, before the docudrama of her life is ever produced. But more than that, her docudrama is completely mundane and predictable. Her story makes the extraordinary (a woman's multiple murders of men) completely ordinary—a homeless prostitute walking the edge without a pimp, she found it more rewarding to turn tricks than be a motel maid, and later found it more lucrative to murder and rob bad johns than to fuck them for $20 or to let them rob or murder *her.* Meanwhile, the legal system and the deductive ratonalizations of popular crime-solving want to make the ordinary fragments of Wuornos's dismembered life into an extraordinary, exotic, and exemplary narrative of crime and punishment.

But what are we re-membering in the story of Aileen Wuornos? Is it that lesbians have real relations to specific forms of social violence? Is it that sometimes it's difficult to tell the police from the bad johns, the honest men from the dishonest men, problematized in the made-for-TV movie by the undercover cop who both befriends Wuornos and betrays her, or by the dead johns who turn out to be a minister and a state social worker? Is it that Wuornos is the embodiment of social violence—as homeless woman, incest "survivor," rape and robbery victim, highway prostitute, and "killer dyke"? Is it the symptomatology of postincest "profile" in her story: suicide attempt, self-hatred, anger, repression, multiple personalities, loss of family, and the loss of economic stability that accompanies loss of family?

Are we re-membering the primal scene of the bad john being shot in the heart, brain, and genitals by a highway prostitute that he tried to "rob"— killed in the Florida woods already signed by the deracination of the Seminoles, by the economically condoned social violence against migrant labor, and by the overt oppression of poverty-stricken African Americans, Hispanic Americans, Mexicans, Haitians, Jamaicans, and others?[1] Is it that Wuornos is the blond white woman, the other other of *Paris Is Burning* (1991), poor white trash killing the offending family members, the incestuous grandfather and uncle, over and over and over? Is it the signature of repetition and death drive, not finally interiorized as self-mutilation and suicide so common to femininity's contemporary signature, but exteriorized as the seriated murder of the other?

Are we re-membering the coldness and cruelty she learned from the absent mother who abandoned her and who was also a victim of domestic violence, and from the father imprisoned for child molestation who hung himself in prison—two generations of angry knowledge passed down as a sociopsychological and physiological body of signs, body memories, and night terrors? Is it that popular images of "killer dykes" provide a convenient screen memory for the massive workings of terror and violence of the killing-machine? Or is it that Wuornos, signing herself as the daughter at the bottom of the bottom of the white social hierarchy, is the last whipping post, the place where the buck stops, finally, as a storm of meaningless violences, flights of desperation, alcohol, outrage, alienation, and schizonoia— "the last resort" of illegitimate identity, like the bar bearing that name where Wuornos was finally arrested (MacNamara)?

As homeless lesbian prostitute, Wuornos is beyond the protection of the nuclear family and the law. Without men to threaten retribution, she takes revenge into her own hands, but in doing so she is marked always and already as the victim, the scapegoat, and the sacrificial body. Theoretically, a just legal system can fill the gap of a missing family narrative, but we know, as does she, that that belief is only an abstraction. In actuality, Wuornos is alone in the woods with her johns beyond the protection of an abstract law that can only sign itself through the criminalization of her social body, and hers alone—not her grandfather's, not the bodies of her abusive tricks. She can only be known as a visible, intelligible body within the public sphere by the criminalization of her seriature as not suicide and not sacrifice. If she had been the streetwalker murdered in the woods by one of her tricks, or if her early suicide attempt had been successful, Wuornos's signature would have remained forever invisible to the public sphere that, in theory, bears the responsibility for mitigating the violence of inequivalencies within civil society and guaranteeing abstract justice for all citizens (Habermas).

If the difference of Wuornos's sacrificial sign becomes her lesbianism in the popular imaginary (which it has), then the contagion of violence will spread (which it is, increasing the level of violences channeled onto the lesbian social body at large). But let us not forget that the real difference driving Wuornos's life story is her poverty, her economic oppression, her alienation through loss of family typical of adult women subjected to incest as children, her liminal social status as homeless highway prostitute—all that which is uncannily familiar in her story, mundane, completely ordinary, and understandable, that is, her lifetime exposure to un-adulterated forms of "pure" social violence.

That she has a lesbian lover is merely a tender spot in a horrible and sordid sequence of events that constitute the limit-text of her life story. It is the one amorous act of volition that stands counter to her only other act of will that can constitute a signature of her agency as one who refuses victimization — the murder of the other who would Other her. As such, her lesbianism is not the key but the tangential detail of the seriated narrative that must be exoticized by the mass-mediated killing-machine — that is, made extraordinary, but only as cliché, even as its real difference is exorcised, screened, and erased. In the end, expertly worked over by the state police force and under threat of criminal charges, the lover Tyria Moore is led to testify against Wuornos in court — the final betrayal in a long list of betrayals by those who were supposed to "love" her — and the successful rupture of any potential collective lesbian social identity. Understanding the mechanism of Wuornos's lifelong alienation — the systematic reification of all her social relations into relations of violence authorized by regimes of paternal property or commodity exchange on one hand, and the erasure of her illegitimate and unofficial but self-determined relations on the other — Arlene Pralle, a "stranger" who like Wuornos was adopted as an infant, states to the press, "There but by the grace of God I would be." Pralle adopts Wuornos after her imprisonment, thereby inscribing in the public sphere for Wuornos, and all her doubles, at least the signifier of a tangible, permanent, and self-determined social relation that the Law can imprison, but cannot, finally, erase.

Meanwhile, Wuornos's seriature — at the juncture of becoming-lesbian and becoming killing-machine constituting the criminalization of lesbian identity — is time-coded for a feature film, for a few more headlines, for another made-for-TV movie or independent documentary, perhaps, before the chair ends her narrative according to the script she herself wants to write — with a jolt of pure electricity — like the electric circuits of television's simulation of Wuornos's life story. That story is one that she never really had, until TV made it up by giving it at the same time broadcast life, temporal frame, and narrative closure — seriating fragments of a life into mainstream TV that will never add up to either a meaningful story or a just a-judication.

S   I   X

Breakdown

We give our patients toxic substances and must ensure their safety as best we can.
— George Dominiak, M.D. *Psychopharmacology of the Abused*

Nuclear Cells

To speak of the breakdown of rational consciousness and its institutionalizations is to face the task of speaking around the unspeakable, mapping like an archaeologist the premises of a repressed topography under disclosure, knowing all the while that the breakdown will never be found finally in any one place, in any location. Meanwhile, the unspeakable as all that accompanies the breakdown of rational consciousness flows constantly around us, in waves of recollection and amnesia, in peaks and troughs of (dis)closure and repression, in the amplitudes and frequencies of exposure and concealment. This flow is modulated by any number of institutionalized suppression mechanisms for which the breakdown functions as the successful failure of feminine subjectification—the *anti*production of feminine subjectivities. Beyond the unspeakable, only morbid symptoms remain to be located, recovered, mapped—the bulimic vomiting of the toxic maternal, the anorectic refusal to take in the phallus, the neurasthenic introjection of the social feminine as slow suicide, the autistic refusal of the social body as "real" percept through sensory mutilation—mnemic signs providing both clues and impenetrable screens for affects and events present but unrepresentable.

Within the politics of channel/surge/suppress common to the production and antiproduction of feminine social subjects and their self-representation, psychiatric and psychotherapeutic interpretations of the breakdown's mnemic signs function as a mechanism of surge suppression. The hermeneutic practice of diagnosis screens the breakdown's machinic social function with the belief that individual subjects have signed these symptoms, that a central nervous system has produced them. The breakdown both discloses the limit of this belief and provides the scene, and the bodies, for its production. The breakdown (dis)locates the subject in the turbulence between body mnemonics and the machinic mnemonics of the social, between the workings of the organic body and the social constructions of the face and its social landscapes. In the scenario of the breakdown and its aftermath, "recovery" territorializes for the social the breakdown's deterritorialized zones, relocating the subject within a zone of functionality and intelligibility while screening the machinic workings of various social institutions. Between the politics of interpretation and the institution of "mental health," recovery discourse and mental health therapy perform a modulating function in a politics of memory, affect, and desire contained at the level of the individual subject.[1]

While the breakdown is represented in our culture as an event occuring within the individual, nowhere is the abstract social organization of the feminine more apparent than in the moment of its breakdown. A daunting creature when all her systems run, she is a hyperthymic overachiever, technologically loaded with electronic-prosthetic memory, neurochemical-prosthetic personality, and media-prosthetic desires. But breakdowns are common, and when they happen, one can glimpse the (dys)functional organs ordering her as a feminine social subject. She typically drives too fast while complaining of being driven, consumes too much while rushing to the toilet to throw up. Sometimes she acts out. Often she is chronically "depressed," not to mention psychoneurologically wired for psychosis.

The feminine is an abstract-machine and as such precedes any concrete actualization of potential conjunctions between sign-flow and matter-flow in the process of subjectification.[2] Like all abstract assemblages, the feminine as an intelligible social category regulates and channels the flux of signs and things into individuated forms of feminine social being. And in doing so, it regularly produces "dysfunctional" subjectivities—enough of them in fact to stimulate "mental health"

Hereisthehouseitisgreenandwhiteithasareddooritisverypretty
hereisthefamilymotherfatherdickandJaneliveinthegreenandw
hitehousetheyareveryhappyseejaneshehasareddressshewants

*toplaywhowillplaywithjaneseethecatitgoesmeowmeowcomea
ndplaycomeplaywithjanethekittenwillnotplayseemothermoth
erisverynicemotherwillyouplaywithjanemotherlaughslaughm
otherlaughseefatherheisbigandstrongfatherwillyouplaywithja
nefatherissmilingsmilefathersmileseethedogbowwowgoesthe
dogdoyouwanttoplaydoyouwanttoplaywithjaneseethedogrun
rundogrunlooklookherecomesafriendthefriendwillplaywithja
netheywillplayagoodgameplayjaneplay*

— *Toni Morrison*
The Bluest Eye

and psychopharmacology as growth industries in a period of low-growth economics. Indeed, the programming of mood, personality, and affect at the level of brain chemistry has become one of the major markets in the 1990s in the United States, as demonstrated by Eli Lilly's multibillion-dollar profit from the popular antidepressant Prozac.

Though abstract, the organization of signs constituting "the feminine" produces concrete histories that organize and regulate actual social relations and the material substance of expression of social identities. Just as inorganic matter is constantly being abstracted into legitimate forms of social expression through various production practices, so the abstract feminine is always becoming concretely embodied in the organic bodies that constitute the social. All too often that embodiment amounts to an experience of private pain if not sheer terror.

Terror works through the delusion that it exists only elsewhere, at the margins, or in the spectacle of excessive, obsessional violence at home, in the exceptional event, in the psychotic's hallucinatory acting out. But terror is always already at home in the everyday flow of business as usual—a characteristic which Michael Taussig in his extensive writings on the topic sums up in the phrase "terror as usual."[3] This constant if discontinuous state of terror flowing through the social body is what Taussig (1992) terms the "Nervous System"—a system that screens itself with the illusion of a nerve center and hierarchy of control within the individual self, a system that makes hermeneutics its property while projecting it as the property of the individual subject (1). The nervous system is the historical outcome of a legacy of disorganized violences veiled as organized progress by modernity's ideology of an ordered machinic socius. As such, it now energizes a postmodern regime of arbitrariness and planning in the post-World War II reconfiguration of state, market, and transnational corporations (17). The terror that the nervous system both produces and consumes in order to mobilize its workings is hardly confined to the public sphere, much less to foreign borders, however much network news suggests that it is. It pervades the domestic spaces of private life and family life, at home as much as abroad. It enters the psychic space of individuated subjectivity, not a terror without (always we try to keep terror outside, *other*) but a terror within, though continuously in need of projection onto some exteriorized space, all the more so when it hits close to home, in the "aberrations" of abuse (sexual, domestic, emotional, physical, child, substance), of madness and insanity (psychopathology), of suicidality. Through the subjection of the self—its ideation, affect, and behavior—to the cultural category of "mental health" and to the laws of logico-rational thought embodied in the marketplace, the nervous system reterritorializes the "private" interiors of psychic life.

Russ Rhymer's account of an abused girl's flight from silence and back in *Genie* (1993) illustrates how "at home" terror really is. Genie's "case" also tells us that we cannot really speak of the subject's direct experience of the unspeakable that drives the breakdown. In the case of Genie, the breakdown of logico-rational subjectification embodied at the level of the individual comes in the form of emotional and physical violence within the (dys)functional suburban family. Genie as the abused daughter introjects the social as manifestly a system of terror and incorporates that terror as silent pain, dementia, psychoneurological reorganization, and self-mutilation. Encouraged by media sensationalism, we might like to imagine that if we were to go back to that white California suburb, to the house on Golden West Avenue, to that room, its shades perpetually drawn, where a man dressed always in khakis kept his unclothed daughter silently harnessed to an infant potty chair for thirteen and a half years, back to the locked door where he would stand barking and growling at her in the dark—if we could go back there and open that door, maybe we would find some answer. But all we would find would be "Genie"—a matrix of symptoms written on the traumatized body and mind of a girl, signing the limitless, potential inhumanity of so-called human nature. As much as we might try, we can never open such a crypt, never decode such a cipher, it will never speak to us; we can only perhaps feel its affect.

In fact, opening that door would tell us nothing finally of more significance than what the rest of Genie's story makes manifest about how terror reproduces and screens itself. Despite becoming a research "event" in the annals of psycho- and neurolinguistics, thus providing the object of rationalization for several years of grant funding, the girl that science named "Genie" never recovered. Not surprisingly, her story is not so extraordinary after all, but rather common in what it recounts of the failure of the academic sciences as much as of the domestic social fabric. Once Genie's case failed to garner further grant monies from the National Institute of Mental Health, she was returned to the care of the state and placed in a series of foster homes, some abusive, until finally she was returned to the same house where she had passed her childhood imprisoned, silenced, and terrorized, to live out her life with her equally traumatized and impoverished mother, sans the husband/father who shot himself in the temple on the living room floor before he could be taken to trial. Justice failed.

Genie, after a short period in which she learned to speak three-word sentences for an audience of academics, returned eventually to a world of silent pain. What was there to say after all that, anyway? She had been "rescued" in November 1970 from her prison-home, becoming the spectacular case of a girl "trapped in a twentieth-century American suburban bedroom," only to enter a world marked that week by the acquittal of the My Lai massacre soldiers and the bombing of Hanoi (65). Indeed, what made Genie's case a proper object of study for the academic sciences as they were constituted in 1970 was her inability to acquire language and the question of whether that inability was neurobiologically encoded or environmentally learned—not her symptomatic signature as a subject traumatized by terror at home.

Even back in the 1950s, I was used to seeing children's X rays of strange combinations of injuries, what we have come to call unassociated fractures: healing fractures of long bones with subdural fractures of the skull. We didn't know what we were seeing. We were just becoming aware of physical abuse of children, and not psychological, and certainly not sexual—that was still taboo.

—*Howard Hansen M.D., Head of Psychiatry, Children's Hospital*
Genie: An Abused Child's Flight from Silence

As a sufferer of trauma, Genie presented symptoms resembling "shell shock" first noted among veterans of World War I, symptoms now identified within clinical psychology as "posttraumatic stress syndrome." And in this chain of significations leading from exterior frontiers of manifest and ordained violence to domestic interiorities of "unauthorized" violence, it is hardly insignificant that Genie's psychotic father was himself a World War II veteran who later made his living as a machinist in the California aircraft industry—an industry structured on the model of a pyramidal, hierarchical military organization. Commander-in-chief, martial law enforcer, prison guard, Genie's father ran a tight ship at home, imposing on the domestic sphere the order of a barracks: Genie slept in her locked room zipped into a sleeping bag in an oversized crib with wire meshing on the sides and top; her older brother slept on a pallet on the living room floor. Daddy slept every night on the living room recliner, armed, his recliner facing the blank monitor of a television set whose circuitry had long ago become dysfunctional. The master bedroom remained unused—a sealed crypt kept as a shrine to the deceased paternal mater, a flamboyant and independent woman whom Genie's father both adored and hated. Genie's case—billed in psycholinguistics as the historic case of a modern day "wild child"—was really only a story of terror at home, a story less spectacular but far more common than the bombing of the World Trade Center.

       I recount Genie's story here because for me she epitomizes both the pathological production of femininity and the production of femininity as pathology. Her double bind was that to adapt to the flow of terror passing through her home, to go on being in that suburban bedroom, meant to adapt in a social space in which there was no adaptation that was not "maladaptation." While the expression of this double bind was extreme in Genie's case, we would do an injustice to the girl whose (anti)signature exceeds the limit of the psychological case study if we failed to recognize the dilemma of (mal)adaptation and (dys)function as paradigmatic of the state of being feminine in postmodern culture. What Genie's "case" tells us is no revelation—femininity becomes disordered if not pathological in order to adapt to a pathological and disordered socialization. Genie is only one instance of suburban feminine breakdown, but her story makes visible the frightening social fact that femininity as a cultural category is constituted partly as a potentiality for receiving and signing the flow of social violences, that the feminine position is constituted as such within a nervous system producing women as victims/survivors, self-mutilators, dysfunctionals, and designated crazies. Within that ground of being, to adapt (to not suicide) is to (mal)adapt. And the potentialities of that (mal)adaptation are subject to any number of policing and surveillance mechanisms typically organized around suppressing and channeling the relation between memory and affect in the antiproduction of desire.

       Within the nervous system, remembering the past, let alone remembering your dreams or finding your "self," can be a complicated maneuver indeed. Lacking a central organ of regulation and surveillance, the nervous system is composed of a field of surge suppressors distributed throughout its circuitry that function to modulate sign-flux and material-flux as they interface in the production of subjectivity. Surge suppressors organize circuits of social power at the level of the micropolitics of the subject. They work coterminously with macropolitical dimensions of institutional and economic systems by distributing points of subjectification and by localizing sign production. In this function, surge suppressors regulate both the strategic failure of subjectification (the antiproduction of the subject) and the successful (i.e., culturally intelligible) encoding of it. A given point of subjectification is subject to any number of surge suppression systems for modulating the turbulence that continuously runs through it. At the level of the micropolitics of the subject, power is distributed within the nervous system through the production and suppression of the two planes

"I'll never be too old to sit on Daddy's lap."

Informant, Father-Daughter Incest

constituting social being, a plane of subjectification and a plane of *signifiance,* and through the regulation of their relation, that is, the relation of *self* and *meaning*— the domains of memory (as the personal relation to history), affect (as the transduction of asignifying velocities across bodies), and desire (as the assemblage of intensities of being and becoming).

The social subject's physical body and the social subject's nonorganic desiring body are points of localization for the channeling and modulation of memory and affect, as both signification and subjectification are mapped through the body and its imaginary productions and counterproductions of desire. Surge suppression systems thus articulate both around the subject's desiring body—her desiring-machine, her body-without-organs as a nonorganic body of intensities—and about her physical, organic body's systems of interiorization and incorporation—the alimentary, the sexual, the perceptual. Each system of interiorization includes orifices capable of constituting and regulating (or not) borders/flows between inside and outside, between the subject and the social, between self and other. The anorectic and the autistic, for example, deterritorialize their orifices for themselves and against the social, just as Genie competes first with her father and later with the research institution to deterritorialize her mouth, urethra, and anus for her own desire.[4]

Subject to extensive cultural mapping, the body's organic systems are potentially always symptomatic—all the more so in moments when the economy of representation that screens the body's social organization fails. Genie's speech, her organ of social exchange and the voice of her desire, was short-circuited, her experience of terror made neurolinguistically unspeakable (she suffered left-hemisphere dysfunction, though her brain was neurologically intact) first by her father's corporal and corporeal punishment for all vocalization, later by the bureaucratic demands of the research institution that, by not registering the socioemotional aspects of her

What Genie Spoke after Being Rescued

stoppitstoppitstoppitstoppitstoppitstoppitstoppitstoppitstoppitstoppitstoppitstoppitstoppits
toppitstoppitstoppitstoppitstoppitstoppitstoppitstoppitstoppitstoppitstoppitstoppitstoppitsto
PPITSTOPPITSTOPPITSTOPPITSTOPPITSTOPPITSTOPPITSTOPPITSTOPPITS
TOPPITSTOPPITSTOPPITSTOPPITSTOPPITSTOPPITSTOPPITSTOPPITSTO
PPITSTOPPITSTOPPITSTOPPITSTOPPITSTOPPITSTOPPITSTOPPITST
OPPITSTOPPITSTOPPITSTOPPITSTOPPITSTOPPITSTOPPITSTOPSTO
PPITSTOPPITSTOPPITSTOPPITSTOPPITSTOPITSTOPPITSTOP
PITSTOPPITSTOPPITstoppitstoppitstoppitstoppitstoppitstoppitstoppitstoppit
ppitstoppitstoppitstoppitstoppitstoppitstoppitstoppitstoppitstop

stoppit.

—Russ Rhymer,
Genie: An Abused Child's Flight from Silence

experience, perpetuated the terror in Genie's life and facilitated her voluntary emotional and neurobiological shutdown.

Certainly, Genie's "voice," the organ of expression for her affect and desire, was encoded in her symptomatic signature of frustration, as well as in her attachment and control issues common to sufferers of long-enduring traumatic stress.[5] And here we begin to glimpse the workings of the nervous system's everyday violence, for while Genie's researchers reported in symposium papers that frustration was the "only clear affective behavior we could discern," no one attributed any agency to Genie's affect. Thus, nothing was done to relieve frustrating stressors in her environment, which certainly included the research investigators themselves and the rigorous neurological and linguistic testing procedures that accompanied them (41). (Many researchers observed that Genie had to be the most tested child in the history of science.) Sadly, Genie was isolated from the only person, Jean Butler, who attempted to reduce those stressors and from the only noncoercive primary attachment she ever formed with anyone. Though Jean Butler was Genie's teacher at Children's Hospital and though she had Genie live at home with her for a short time, she was denied permanent foster parent status because she was a single woman (officials thought it important that Genie have a father figure in her life) and openly hostile to the intrusions of scientific researchers and careerist academics into the space and time of Genie's healing process. Instead, Genie was placed in the home of David Rigler, the principal investigator of the National Institute of Mental Health research grant awarded to study Genie's language acquisition, in spite of the fact that the Rigler household included a dog, the object of "severe phobia" for the child haunted by memories of a father who barked and growled at her from behind a locked door.[6] Genie regressed. But not as much as she would regress later, upon leaving the Rigler home for more typical foster home environments. By the time she was returned to her mother and the house on Golden West Avenue, she had become once again speechless.

Like the function of Genie's "language acquisition study" in suppressing the surge of suburban breakdown into the community at large, "abuse" discourse serves a monitoring function for the general state of terror pulsating through the nervous system's agitated social body. The politics of interpretation and representation manifested in Genie's case organize and veil the uneven distribution of power across social strata, producing an order of signs that functions like a circuit breaker, monitoring the breakdown's potential to introduce deterritorializing flux into the flow of everyday social meanings.

This economy of representation, with its contingent politics of interpretation, works like a surge suppressor to protect against deterritorializing sign-flows that accompany the breakdown of rational cognition and behavior. Surge suppressors inscribe within the social body a micropolitics of the subject by encoding individuated subjectivities onto abstract social-machines (Guattari 97). In Genie's case, individuation is repeatedly mapped onto the abstract idea of the nuclear family. For example, the research committee refuses Jean Butler's foster parent application based on the assumption that Genie needed a "father figure" in her life. Later, the state returns Genie to her mother and the original scene of her trauma, the house on Golden West Avenue, on the assumption that the mother-daughter bond, even given the unusual circumstances, was the most significant social relation Genie could have.

Perhaps the most disturbing example of projecting an individual subject onto the machinic workings of an institution was the encoding of Genie's individuation onto the abstract machine of scientific research, manifested by the research group's assumption of and insistence upon the presence of Genie's individual subjectivity (even in the face of her missing language organ) in the execution of their research.[7]

GO WHERE PEOPLE SLEEP AND SEE IF THEY'RE SAFE

—Jenny Holzer,
"Survival," from The Venice Installation

The discourse of research produced "Genie" as willing participant rather than human specimen suffering the same loss of volition as a baboon in a scientific experiment. Furthermore, the American suburban household and its dysfunctions at large were never the object of study deserving of research funding. Rather, "Genie," as an embodied individual identity no matter how socially or sensorially "deprived," was the appropriate "subject" for study within the psychosocial sciences.

Genie's story, however, reminds us that the breakdown always comes from within the social, not without, at the same time that its etiology arises not from within the "individual" subject, where psychotherapy would locate it, but from without her, beyond her, in the fabric of her social relations and their normative reification as object-relations. Thus, the reterritorialization of the breakdown within the individual psyche is manifestly a scene of political pragmatics and of capitalist market development, most recently in the form of the burgeoning industry of psychopharmacology. While countries like Japan are developing high-tech products for the world market, the United States is capitalizing on its own depressed and disordered citizenry, turning a profit off disorder-treatment drugs such as Prozac, Ritalin, and Zoloft—products of the merger between psychiatry and the pharmaceutical industry after World War II.

An abstract suppression-machine, psychopharmacology constitutes a material practice in the treatment of posttraumatic stress syndrome, major depression, manic-depression, borderline and multiple personality disorder, psychoses, and more and more frequently of late, minor depression and anxiety, funk and malaise. Women are a large proportion of the psychopharmacological market; most of those taking the antidepressant Prozac, for example, are women in their childbearing years (Stone 91). Because memory is emotional-state dependent, psychotropic interventions in and modulations of feminine affect produce at a neurobiological level a gendered chemical prosthetic subject whose repressed memories of the nervous system's circulating violences are the object of channeling, regulation, research, and development. The psychopharmaceutical industry's general economy channels repressed memories of the nervous system's unspeakable yet everyday terror and modulates their return as emotional and psychic disorders.[8] Where psychotherapy modulates collective memory at the molecular level by keeping articulated memories sequestered in the private space of the clinician's office, psychopharmacology has brought a new level of understanding to the meaning of molecular politics. Working at the level of particle-signs where they are generated neurologically within the organic body, neurochemical interventions reterritorialize the molecular assemblage of limbic and autonomic particle-signs into blocks of memory, organized emotional expressions, and continuums of desiring-intensities. In short, neurochemical interventions both reterritorialize and stabilize blocks of becoming.

According to Guattari (1984), the plane of consistency where a micropolitics of desire could articulate would include any mechanisms, whether biochemical, social, or machinic, that stabilize deterritorializations between social content and the machinic expression of form. His term *desiring-machine* is meant to suggest the workings of an abstract expression-machine in the process of stabilizing deterritorializations of desire: "The non-signifying expression machine (on the level of the signifier) organizes a system of empty words and interchangeability for all the territorialized systems of words produced by the manifold local agencies of power. (We may instance the power of the family over the production of nice speech, or the power of the school over the production of nice writing, discipline, competition, hierarchy, etc.)" (83). For Deleuze (1993), who favors the term "assemblage" to "machine," the key to understanding the mapping of power onto desire is to understand that "desire only exists when assembled or machined" (136). The point then is to ask not to which drives desires correspond, but to ask into which assemblage various blocks of becoming enter. There are different politics of assemblages, and psychopharmacology's expression-machine can enter into relations with any number of them. Desire does not precede its social construction. Likewise, the plane of consistency articulating an assemblage of signatory and social relations does not precede the assemblage but is constituted by it (137). Since all assemblages are socially constructed, all assemblages inscribe a politics. The politics of biopsychiatry, because biopsychiatry works at the level of the individual's brain chemicals, is expressed as a neural micropolitics.

In this micropolitics, the components of desire are reterritorialized through a psychochemical-machine whose delivery system is psychiatric diagnosis and prescription of psychotropic drugs. The components for potential desiring-assemblages include repressed memory (interiorized expressions of impressions and experiences that lack exteriorized forms of expression) and the resulting surges of repressed affect (deterritorializing velocities of asignification traversing the body's limbic system). Psychotropic medications actualize potential conjunctions between abstract systems of rational cognition and behavior and material social systems organizing a technologically and economically striated domestic space, workplace, and institutional space.

On a biochemical plane of articulation, psychotropic intervention shapes an abstract feminine chemical prosthetic subject by modulating deterritorializing surges within the nervous system at the level of the micropolitics of the subject. In the flow of rational consciousness both within the individuated subject and within the social body at large, *surge* can be understood as what a particular point of subjectification experiences in relation to turbulent social force. In the collective movement of particle-signs that constitutes the flow of rational significations, surge-flux threatens to change the rate or direction of the sign-flow of established meanings. In terms of the breakdown, surges of desire, affect, and memory express as the frequency and amplitude of symptoms and symptom clusters, with frequency expressing as the measure of sign-flux passing through its cycle of occurrence (marking the duration and relation of affective events) and amplitude expressing as emotional intensity. Neurochemical treatments reterritorialize the frequencies and amplitudes of flux, that is, the temporality, spatiality, and intensity of the feminine subject's neural network assembling affect, memory, and desire into meaningful and intense blocks of becoming. Directing flows of signs within the social body, psychopharmacology channels asignifications within the body politic onto the individual subject's wired and rewired affect. Within this juncture of psychopathology and pharmacology, the politics of interpretation takes the formal expression of the science of symptomatology—a practice that is in actuality a virtual hermeneutic nightmare.

Within clinical psychology, the recent articulation of a domestic "posttraumatic stress disorder" provides a paradigmatic example of this interpretive nightmare and its political implications, while demonstrating the way the nervous system expresses itself and recuperates its effects through the bodies of individual subjects and their breakdowns. The now accepted clinical practice of diagnosing posttraumatic stress disorder in cases of domestic and sexual abuse simultaneously recognizes the nervous system's circulating violences on the home front and screens the nervous system's everyday effects with a discourse of psychopathology (Herman 1992). Common clinical symptoms of adults suffering from posttraumatic stress disorder, when the "trauma-stress" was experienced within the domestic household early in their social becoming, are alarmingly profuse. They include acting out,[9] blurred boundaries, body image disturbance, chemical dependency, cognitive deficits, depression, dissociation, eating disorders, emotional numbing, fear/paranoia, flashbacks, hearing inner voices, hypnagogic hallucinations, inability to trust, insomnia, low self-esteem, minimizing, multiple and borderline personality, persistent anxiety, promiscuity, reactive affective states, recurrent nightmares, sexual dysfunction, self-injurious behavior, somatization, and suicidality. The syndrome is often characterized by an incubation period of anywhere from ten to thirty years. If this "disorder" is as pervasive as the general effects of the nervous system, we can only speculate how "normative" the syndrome—which is quickly becoming *the* psychological disorder of the 1990s—actually is. Indeed, once it was recognized formally within clinical psychology, posttraumatic stress disorder began to challenge the legitimacy of many previous clinical diagnostic practices and psychopathological classifications.

In fact, clinical researchers and practitioners agree on only one thing in cases of posttraumatic stress syndrome. As one expert in the field put it, "For traumatized individuals, many of the usual assumptions about symptoms do not apply. For example, the presence of hallucinations may not indicate psychosis, depression may not be major affective disorder, episodic overwhelming anxiety may not be panic, and hypomanic agitation may not be bipolar disorder" (Dominiak 89). The task of diagnosing and treating a syndrome with a variable, multisymptom, and malleable presentation makes determination of "medication-responsive primary major psychiatric illness," "symptom management," and "appropriate pharmacologic intervention" an unstable procedure at best. Yet, currently diagnosis and treatment occur in a milieu in which one-half of all patients who seek assistance from the psychiatric institution are treated pharmacologically (U.S. Department of Health and Human Services). Because symptoms of posttraumatic stress disorder can mimic borderline states, lethal crises, and psychotic reactions, clinicians are faced with the challenge of distinguishing "agitation from hypomania, and psychosis from dissociation, other forms of dyscontrol, and abreaction" (Dominiak 108).

Everything is at stake in the initial diagnosis, since dissociation, the fragmenting of thought processes (i.e., *suppression*), is recognized as an appropriate defense mechanism *against* psychosis in situations of enduring traumatic stress, while abreaction, defined as the release of repressed emotions by acting out in words, action, or imagination the situation causing the conflict (i.e., *surge*), is identified by most clinicians working with posttraumatic stress syndrome as a crucial step in the recuperative process for traumatized individuals (108). This core contradiction within the regime of signs expressing as psychopathological diagnosis and "symptom management" generates breakdowns of its own, since the psychic process that defends *against* psychosis looks like psychosis. *Surge* signs simultaneously as healing process and as the "maladaptive" symptom authorizing the neurochemical policing of memory, affect, and desire. Indeed, treating abreactive surges of affect pharmacologically requires drastic amounts of sedation that not only debilitate and slow the subject in her therapeutic work but typically prove entirely ineffective in the long run in relieving the violent return of repressed and fragmented emotion and memory (108). Needless to say, being diagnosed and treated pharmacologically for psychosis when you are not yet psychotic is antitherapeutic.

Surge (Suppressor)

The standard protocol for psychiatric diagnosis—determination of the patient's symptomatology as either psychotic or nonpsychotic and the decision to use only psychosocial intervention or to medicate—is challenged by the variable symptom cluster of posttraumatic stress disorder, since posttraumatic stress disorder's plane of consistency crosses many previous diagnostic categories. Clinical practitioners face the daily hermeneutic dilemma of distinguishing psychotic phenomena from symptoms that may appear to be psychosis but are instead "attributable to dissociation, splitting, intrusive thoughts, vivid recollections, obsessionality, and extreme emotional reactions" (98). The distinction between functionality and dysfunctionality, which often determines more radical psychotropic intervention, is described by one clinician as the point at which adaptive defense mechanisms become "overly rigid" or "exaggerated" (Shapiro 35).

In addition, the clinical judgment distinguishing between psychopathological dysfunction and adaptive functionality is subject to codes of class and social status. For example, the environmental supports of the patient, including familial, social, and financial resources, are standard criteria for psychopharmacological evaluation, along with the individual's psychiatric assessment (Dominiak 108). By this standard of evaluation, the underclasses would be by definition more prone to psychotropic treatments than nonpharmaceutical ones. It is no surprise that the psychiatric network finds it easier and more efficacious to diagnose mental illness and prescribe medication than to bolster social and familial resources for the poor. In regard to mental illness among socioeconomically "underprivileged" populations, the blurred boundary between adaptation and maladaptation is at its most acute, while the political stakes invested in first producing and then channeling collective (mal)adaptations become most tangible.

Canguilhem's extensive critique of the categories of normality and normativity in *The Normal and the Pathological* frame this problem of diagnosis in the context of a broader understanding of health:

The normal should not be opposed to the pathological, because under certain conditions and in its own way, the pathological is normal. . . . Health is more than normality; in simple terms, it is normativity. Behind all apparent normality, one must look to see if it is capable of tolerating infractions of the norm, of overcoming contradictions, of dealing with conflicts. Any normality open to possible future correction is authentic normativity, or health. Any normality limited to maintaining itself, hostile to any variation in the themes that express it, and incapable of adapting to new situations is a normality devoid of normative intention.
When confronted with any apparently normal situation, it is therefore important to ask whether the norms that it embodies are creative norms, norms with a forward thrust, or, on the contrary, conservative norms, norms whose thrust is toward the past. (352)

One must distinguish, therefore, between the "pathological normal" and the "normative normal" (352). And in making this distinction, one inevitably confronts a politics of normality. In this regard, the pathology of normality cannot help but be a politics of normality.[10] And a politics of normality is not the same thing as health.

This politics of diagnostic hermeneutics is particularly manifest in diagnoses of *borderline personality disorder,* a term formally used within psychopathology to designate "troubles lying on the frontier between neurosis and psychosis, particularly latent schizophrenias presenting an apparently neurotic set of symptoms" (Laplanche and Pontalis 54). The semiotic terrain of borderline disorder is ambiguous at best, repressive at worst. The psychosocial etiology of the disorder is admittedly diffuse and subject to multiple determinations. Clinical research in psychopathology has shown not only childhood trauma but chronic stress to be potential antecedents of borderline personality disorder (Shapiro 2). Borderline personality disorder as a diagnostic category is broad, inclusive, and vague. It constitutes the official "gray" area between neurosis and psychosis, between psychosocial treatment and psychotropic medication, between outpatient treatment and institutionalization in

Tess was someone who came from a poor working-class background, who was able to have some of that injury reversed through medication.

—Peter Kramer,
author of Listening to Prozac.[11]

the practice of psychiatry. Susanna Kaysen, author of *Girl, Interrupted* (1993), an autobiographical account of her psychiatric institutionalization at age seventeen, was classified as having borderline personality disorder. On looking up the classification in the *Diagnostic and Statistical Manual of Mental Disorders* twenty-five years after her discharge, Kaysen found this gloss: "This is often pervasive and is manifested by un-certainty about several life issues, such as self-image, sexual orientation, long-term goals or career choice, types of friends or lovers to have, and which values to adopt" (150).

Kaysen comments in her moving account that "often an entire family is crazy, but since an entire family can't go into the hospital, one person is designated as crazy and goes inside" (95). One is hardly surprised that in Kaysen's family, the designated crazy is the disturbed daughter. The social limit of insanity, however, hardly ends with the family. Not only is the individuation of psychopathol-ogy within psychiatry a suppression system for the nervous system at large, but the oedipalization of the subject in psychoanalysis and psychotherapy, that is, the re-duction of the identity and meaning of the social subject to her familial history, is a suppression of group psychosis and general dysfunction within the socius. Psycho-pathology as it is currently practiced suppresses the need for group psychiatry, so-ciohistorical analysis, and the integration of the subject's history with the group's history.[12] On the battlefront of desire, where points of subjectification localize both sign production and the production of subjectivity, "For desire to be expressed in individual terms means that it is already condemned to castration" (Guattari 72).

The discourse of psychopathology, technologized in its postmod-ern form as psychopharmacology, reproduces the distributional flow of social power by suppressing the assemblage of desiring-machines in touch with the historical so-cial experience and memory of the group. Psychopharmacology functions as a *surge*

I became my mother's hell. She called me Dolly, the doll she never had. In her own words I learned who I was: "You were my doll, and I was allowed to smash it," she told me over and over again.

—*Donna Williams*
Nobody Nowhere: The Extraordinary Autobiography of an Autistic

suppressor, putting a brake on flux (any tendency to change direction, speed, or inten-sity) within the collective flow of feminine social bodies and signs. In short, biopsy-chiatry puts a brake on nonmajoritarian desire, which can express within the collective social flow only as *surge*—sudden accelerations of sign-flow away from established meanings. As an interpretative machine, psychopharmacology modulates the po-tential flux in desire and affect caused by historical social memory embodied in the individual subject. The abstract-machine of rationality as it is institutionalized in psy-chopharmacology modulates cognition, behavior, and desire on two planes: neuro-chemical and representational. The neurochemical plane regulates embodied knowledge as the subjective assemblage of memory, affect, and desire; the representational plane regulates the flow of signs between the individual and the public.

On the plane of subjectification in psychopharmacology's double articulation, psychopharmacological treatment rewires the traumatized subject's faciality through a process formally expressed within psychiatry as "symptom management." Symptom management modulates subjectification by deterritorializing potential conjunctions between neurochemical processes and abstract social facialities, working at a neurobiological ground zero of social being and becoming. Psychotropic drugs enter the subject through the organic body, territorializing three neurobiological systems of the brain: the serotonergic system, the limbic system, and the autonomic nervous system.

Each chemical intervention actualizes potential conjunctions between adaptive defensive mechanisms presenting as "maladaptive" symptoms and "normative" (i.e., functional, intelligible, and socially acceptable) ideation, affect, and behavior. For example, episodic violent outbursts associated with anamnesis (surges of recollection) and abreaction (release of repressed emotions) can be regulated with the anticonvulsant carbamazepine (Tegretol). Counterindications of carbamazepine include potentially hazardous side effects on bone marrow and liver, skin rashes, and lightheadedness. Carbamazepine regulates behavorial "dyscontrol" by modulating "epileptoid overactivity" of limbic structures, those parts of the brain responsible for generating emotional experience and memories and for influencing emotion-related behaviors (Dominiak 106). "Emotional storms" produced by asignifying turbulences traversing the individuated and alienated subject can thus be nipped in their neurochemical bud if not in their social context. Angry women overcome by surges of rage and violent acting-out behavior, self-mutilation, and suicidal actions, caught in a cycle of dissociation and intrusive abreaction, can be suppressed at the very neurobiological root of emotion and memory and at the neurochemical point of origin of dissociation.

The most pervasive psychic defense mechanism, dissociation appears across a vast strata of symptomatologies, including schizophrenia, borderline personality disorder, multiple personality disorder, and posttraumatic stress syndrome. Dissociation is generally understood to be "temporary alteration of the general integrative function of consciousness," characterizing states ranging from splitting and psychogenic amnesia to depersonalization and multiple personality (Shapiro 43). Within the micropolitics of subjectification, dissociation can be understood as the demolecularization of memory and affect, the reduction and separation of memory-blocks into simpler groups or single particles, and the deterritorialization of associational affective formations. Dissociation and splitting are the fundamental symptoms of schizophrenia, the term coined by Bleuler in 1911 to designate psychoses characterized by *zerspaltung* (disintegration and fragmentation) and *spaltung* (splitting of thought into two groups) (Laplanche 408). Dissociation can also present as psychogenic amnesia, a symptom historically associated with hysteria (Shapiro 44). While dissociation may well function as an internalized surge-suppression mechanism articulated through the subject's limbic system, in its

> *The social machine's limit is not attrition, but rather its misfirings;*
> *it can operate only by fits and starts, by grinding and breaking down,*
> *in spasms of minor explosions.*
>
> —*Deleuze and Guattari,*
> Anti-Oedipus

extreme forms of expression it becomes itself "pathological" and must, in turn, be suppressed. While antidepressants and anxiolytics (tranquilizers) suppress depression and anxiety, however, they do not affect dissociation. In cases of multiple personality disorder, lithium can be prescribed to suppress pathological dissociation expressed as "switching," though clinicians admit that rewiring multiple personality disorder with psychotropic medication presents the risk of suppressing more regulating personalities and activating "unwanted alters" (Dominiak 103).

In the recently articulated clinical syndrome connecting sexual abuse to posttraumatic stress disorder, popularized and legitimized within the clinical community by Judith Herman's *Trauma and Recovery* (1992), a direct relation has been recognized between experiences of victimization and the presence of dissociation. The clinical recognition of a posttraumatic stress syndrome among the abused disputes Freud's reading of hysteria as a fantasmatic production of incestuous desire on the part of the daughter, and is an initial step toward interpreting "hysterical" symptoms as actual outcomes of the nervous system. In cases of abuse trauma, particularly when the victim is a dependent child, dissociation is seen as an appropriate way for the mind to escape what the social body cannot (Shapiro 44).

What is repressed through dissociation, however, does not remain dormant but returns as a sequelae to abuse trauma: nightmares, memory flooding, somatization, depersonalization, and parasuicidal behavior. In other words, dissociation (*suppression*) expresses in a wave structure with uncontrollable memory (*surge*) appearing in the form of intrusive memories, flashbacks, night terrors, auditory hallucinations, and memory fragments that can generate their own psychic reactions in the fluctuations of surge and suppression. Clinical research in the area of abuse, psychopathology, and psychopharmacology suggests that dissociative states are not usually responsive to neuroleptic intervention in the long run (Dominiak 100), while clinical practice suggests that for all dissociative phenomena, healing involves verbalization and the integrative processing of memories and affect associated with the traumatic stress and its prolonged repression.

While dissociation, understood as the formal expression of the subject's alienation from her own memories and from social representation, cannot be successfully "treated" with neurochemical intervention, the secondary symptoms produced by dissociation are regularly treated with psychotropic medications. Posttraumatic stress disorder, for example, like bipolar disorder, tends to express in a bimodal fluctuation of states of hyperarousal (agitation, anxiety, abreaction, anamnesis, memory flooding, flashbacks, hypomania, micropsychotic breaks, intrusive thoughts or voices, acting out, intense mood shifts, insomnia, self-mutilation, and suicidal behavior) and states of avoidance (splitting, emotional shutdown, fugue states, minimizing, denial, depression). The symptoms associated with each of these states can be treated psychotropically. Propanolol, for example, can be prescribed to suppress autonomic hyperarousal. Complications from propranolol include altered cognitive functioning, depression, delirium, and hypotension (Dominiak 104).

Hyperarousal of the autonomic nervous system, which includes the sympathetic and parasympathetic systems regulating the heart, intestines, and glands, can also be suppressed at the neurochemical level with benzodiazepines, or "tranquilizers." Benzodiazepines can produce side effects of chemically induced amnesia, oversedation, physiological dependence, and enhancement of behavorial dyscontrol if taken with alprazolam (Xanax) and lorazepam (Ativan) (Dominiak 105). The traumatized subject can self-regulate hyperarousal, producing an internal calming effect by stimulating stress-induced analgesia through cutting,

SHRIEK WHEN THE PAIN HITS DURING INTERROGATION. REACH INTO THE DARK AGES TO FIND A SOUND THAT IS LIQUID HORROR, A SOUND OF THE BRINK WHERE MAN STOPS AND THE BEAST AND NAMELESS CRUEL FORCES BEGIN. SCREAM WHEN YOUR LIFE IS THREATENED, FORM A NOISE SO TRUE THAT YOUR TORMENTOR RECOGNIZES IT AS A VOICE THAT LIVES IN HIS OWN THROAT. THE TRUE SOUND TELLS HIM THAT HE CUTS HIS FLESH WHEN HE CUTS YOURS, THAT HE CANNOT THRIVE AFTER HE TORTURES YOU.

—*Jenny Holzer*
"*Inflammatory Essays,*" *from* The Venice Installation

starvation, or head banging. When this circuit of self-regulated psychic pain modulation becomes "pathological," the psychopharmacologist can prescribe naloxone — a receptor blockade with opiate antagonists that suppresses the processing of endogenous opioids, though this intrusive form of chemical intervention (the drug must be delivered intravenously) has shown little long-term effect on subjects whose sphere of psychic and social control has already been reduced to the interiority of their own physical body, as in anorexia and bulimia and other forms of parasuicidal or suicidal self-mutilation (105).

Neural Micropolitics

The abstract-machine of rational cognition and behavior institutionalized by psychopharmacology articulates not only neurochemically on a plane of subjectification but also on a plane of signification by modulating and channeling sign flow in the body politic's economy of representation. Kate Millett's autobiographical account of her institutionalization and placement on lithium for manic-depression, *The Looney-Bin Trip* (1990), provides an example of the workings of psychopharmacology's double articulation. The relation between subjectification and signifiance, between the neurochemical and representational strata of the breakdown's double articulation is rhizomatic.

There are two "incidents" of Millett's "madness." The first incident resulted in institutionalization and lithium treatment. The second incident occurred six years later when she announced her decision to discontinue psychotropic treatment because for her "lithium represented collusion" (95). Both incidents exemplify the institutional antiproduction of Millett's subjectivity as a remembering, thinking, and desiring machine. In the first breakdown, a social field of sign-events becomes localized around Millett's individuated body. On the plane of representation, madness is a signatory slide and as such must be cordoned off, contained at all cost at the level of some one, of some body. Much like Kaysen functioning as the "designated crazy" within her family, Millett becomes the designated crazy within the community. Sign-flux within the body politic is reduced to Millett's personal breakdown and institutionalization. Frantic to assist in a civil rights intervention on behalf of Michael X, a writer and activist eventually hanged illegally in Trinidad, Millett becomes fatigued and hyperactive. Family and friends feel she spends "too much of her own money" flying to England to represent Michael's case to the media on behalf of Michael's wife, who is not allowed in the country. She becomes consumed with the project, giving it "too much of her time." She begins to act "irrationally." At the same time, though married, Millett has fallen in love with a woman, Sita, and does not see her commitment to both relationships as contradictory.

Eventually signed into the psychiatric institution by her family, Millett herself becomes a sign-attractor reordering a destabilizing surge of asignification within the body politic and its ideology of "sanity." On the plane of representation, Millett's breakdown (represented as an asystematic psychotic break within the individual, i.e., insanity) screens the community's collusion in the nervous system's circulating violences, that is, in a manifestly violent social reality, which is signed by the terrorizing injustices channeled to the sacrificial body of Michael X. For Millett, Michael X's unjust execution, coupled with the failure of her personal relations and her own institutionalization, begins a signatory slide that signs the madness of the body politic that her own insanity functions to screen:

But be honest. You've had some moments. The looney-bin trip, the Thorazine, even just the terror.
Everything becomes symbol and significance, echo and gesture, doubles and representatives.
Did you tell yourself that last time it didn't happen or you didn't see it, disbelieved it,
remembered it only blurringly in fleeting recollections as irrationality, embarrassing
grandiose illusions? Like your cavalier comparisons with Joan on the way to the insanity trial—
that must have been it, that was craziness, I'd say to myself. Or confusing the cleaning woman
in the hospital lavatory with Sita; their age, their darkness and humility—
that was crazy. And I would wince that here, surely, was confusion as to persons
and places. The way the black man in solitary at Napa was Michael X,
as all blacks in imprisonment were counters, doubles. (85)

From the point of view of the psychiatric institution, however, the body politic is not insane; Millett is.

Diagnosed as manic-depressive, the "cure" is to place Millett's individuated body on lithium to stabilize her depression and to prevent future "manic" episodes. Once placed on lithium treatment, however, the treatment itself signs Millett as crazy—a sign function that becomes manifest when she announces she is getting off the medication. Suddenly, her actions become suspect and subject to public and private surveillance. She becomes too excitable over another "idealistic" project. Turning a farm into a feminist artists community, she again spends too much money. Struggling over accounts, she becomes insomniac. Discouraged by petty infighting and a creeping lack of vision and commitment among young interns within the community, she becomes irritable and short-tempered. Her judgments are scrutinized for signs of irrationality; she goes to a horse auction to buy a horse and comes home with five horses she cannot really afford because she cannot bear to see them sold to the package-house buyers who, for a small profit, are willing to turn them into so many pounds of dogmeat. Is it not perfectly clear that without lithium Millett risks full-blown insanity? After all, she has already been diagnosed. Friends and family descend upon Millett's New York apartment to "intervene" a second time—armed with a psychiatrist and two psychiatric hospital ambulances replete with strong-armed men with white coats and stretchers. Millett is saved by a black New York City street cop who backs her up—in the state of New York hospitalization without consent is illegal. Had she been in another state or less informed of her rights, she might not have fared so well.

Millett's account exemplifies psychopharmacology's double articulation at work. On the plane of subjectification, lithium is a neurochemical antiproducing Millett's personality by modulating at the organic ground zero of her brain chemistry that which in her desire, articulated in her affect and behavior, causes surges in the communal flow of signs and bodies. On the plane of significance, lithium is an order-word, a sign-attractor, and a retroactive signifier modulating sign-flux within a community of significations screening everyday social violences—including the violence, executed even by family and community in the name of rationality and care, of selectively policing minoritarian bodies and desires.

Millett's personal account of her struggle with "madness" reminds us that the abstract-machine of logico-rationality both produces the breakdown as an outcome of circulating social violences and also capitalizes on its recuperation. The breakdown is both the product of the abstract social machine of logico-rational subjectification (as it is materialized in any number of institutions from the nuclear family and marriage to social services, mental health, and criminal law) and is the trigger mobilizing the workings of the abstract social machinic and its mechanisms of suppression and policing. The breakdown makes this structural double bind manifest. The flow of violences through the nervous system, which cannot keep its violent productions exterior to itself, systematically produces adaptive neuropsychic lines of flight in individual subjects. From the point of view of the socius's politics of representation, however, these adaptive flights are "maladaptive disorders"—major depressive disorder, posttraumatic stress disorder, borderline personality disorder, multiple personality disorder, bipolar disorder, mood disorder, delusional disorder, psychotic disorder.

These (mal)adaptations are then subject to suppression systems modulating both the systematic production of (dys)functional subjectivities and the antiproduction of those subjectivities. In short, desiring intensities are located within individuated social subjects and then modulated through psychic pain and consequent "symptom management," producing a circuit of power that runs off "significantly dysfunctional" lives and the reification of those lives as object-relations. Ironically, the presenting symptoms of (dys)functional disorders are both appropriate adaptations to the environmental stressors of the nervous system and prodromic phases for psychosis. In other words, the nervous system's circulating social violence is the ground zero of psychosis, a fact thinly screened by victimology's study of "vulnerable populations"—children, women, the poor, oppressed minorities, and the insane.

This understanding of psychosis is not antithetical to Kristeva's (1986) reading of aggressivity as unsymbolized drive, as a violence that remains just beyond the economy of representation (237), nor to Lacan's (1993) reading of a psychotic psychical economy in which repression channels a "transitivism of evil intentions" characterizing delusional projections and suggesting a paranoid point of truth of paranoia (Lacan 146). In Lacan's post-Freudian reading, the subject's imaginary comes into being at the moment of her alienation, that is, "the imaginary mechanism gives psychotic alienation its form but not its dynamics" (146). In fact, the consensual "understanding" of signs and meanings constituting rational sanity and supposedly distinguishing psychosis is itself clearly imaginary. There is no structural difference, then, between rational cognition and insanity, between

While I fought with all my strength not to let myself sink in the Enlightenment, I saw things mocking me from their places, taunting me threateningly. And in my head foolish phrases floated around without let-up. I closed my eyes to escape the surrounding turmoil of which I was the center. But I could find no rest, for horrible images assailed me, so vivid that I experienced actual physical sensation. I can not say that I really saw images; they did not represent anything. Rather I felt them. It seemed that my mouth was full of birds which I crunched between my teeth, and their feathers, their blood and broken bones were choking me. Or I saw people whom I had entombed in milk bottles, putrefying, and I was consuming their rotting cadavers. Or I was devouring the head of a cat which meanwhile gnawed at my vitals. It was ghastly, intolerable.

In the midst of this horror and turbulence, I nonetheless carried on my work as a secretary.

—schizophrenic girl, recounted to her analyst Marguerite Sechehaye,
Autobiography of a Schizophrenic Girl

"adaptation" and "maladaptation," a point that Lacan expresses in the provocative statement, "Psychosis is in the place of freedom" (145).

The implications of this premise—that the nervous system's very rationality is the ground zero of psychosis—are vast enough to merit dwelling upon.

Representation will of course get in the way wherever it can, repressing the fact that the nervous system's circulating social violence is pervasive rather than aberrative. But if we recognize "traumatic stress" (understood as a prodromic phase for psychopathology) as the experience of absolute powerlessness, the utter devaluation of personhood in the face of the exercise of authority or power, as one clinical researcher in the field of sexual trauma and psychopathology defines it, then we begin to make visible the effects of the nervous system on the general production of subjectivity within postmodern culture (Dominiak 18).

Within the nervous system, domestic "traumatic stress" is merely a common form of embodied knowledge, introjected by the subject early in her social becoming, in which caring gestures, community leaders, loving family members, and family friends veil a system of terror. And this system of terror is transducted to the child—to the child's desiring body and her biophysical body—as surges within the supposed "safety zone" of home and community, surges of emotional and physical violence, expressed by violation, cruelty, and neglect, either experienced firsthand or witnessed, and responded to by family and community with alienation, complicity, and silence (18).[13] When the silence is broken, the psychiatric system—comprising schools, hospitals, psychiatric medicine, social service programs and insurance companies—a bureaucratic network scathingly critiqued by Louise Armstrong in *And They Call It Help: The Psychiatric Policing of America's Children* (1993), responds to these children who are themselves the product of every conceivable social problem and familial breakdown or to the adults they become by labeling

I can feel it again, the way I did so many years ago.

Bending a Coke can back and forth, back and forth until it tore and made a knife. Cutting myself. Doing it carefully, very carefully, so that just a line of red opened behind my blade's slow progress.

Or a little burn, perhaps, the edge of the iron as I was pressing a skirt for school.

It wasn't masochism so much as a sort of drug. The small, specific sensation, the red color, was calming to me. That strange way pain can make you taste metal in your mouth. Not from licking the blood, that's not what I mean: just a taste that comes into your consciousness along with a smell like ammonia, something you might be thinking rather than sensing. It didn't hurt, not really, it felt.

I didn't know why I did it, not then. But now I do. I longed for a wound that showed.

—*Kathryn Harrison*, Exposure

them mentally ill and subjecting them to drugs, psychotherapy, and institutionalization.

The abstract-machine of mental health (in conjunction with the nuclear family-machine, the couple-machine, the worker-machine) suppresses sign-flux from the representation of the body politic at large by reducing the social space of the breakdown to the "individual" psyche. Within this reduced space, psychopharmacology reterritorializes at the level of neurochemicals the isolated and alienated subject's affect and behavior as components of her desire, in effect articulating not only a micropolitics of desire but also a micropolitics of affect and memory. Clinical psychology has long demonstrated that "behavioral dyscontrol" has a direct relation to affect, and affect has a direct relation to memory processes. Psychopharmacology thus performs a regulatory function, correlating a machinic-affective system and a machinic-mnemonic system by modulating concrete relays between the politics of representation, expressed as diagnostic hermeneutics, and the micropolitics of affect and behavior, expressed as neurochemical relations to "memory events."

For the "traumatized" subject who has introjected an invisible and unspeakable terror, affect becomes a minefield of symptom-signs in a battlefield of surging memories and introjected social structures of mnemonic suppression. The turbulence of the surge and the force of the suppression are all the greater when the trauma-stress occurred in childhood and involved a taboo requiring secrecy, as in domestic violence involving adults and children; physical, sexual, and emotional abuse; incest. From a machinic perspective, affective "mood disorders" can be understood as the failed representation of memory events—failed because the memory events mark points of subjectification that are under surveillance or even erasure by a socialized suppression system. For the woman (the case study calls her "Susan") sitting in a Mexican restaurant when an "acute anxiety attack" overcomes her, what is at stake is not only the state of being of her so-called mental health, but her history as a body of memory-events and the relation of her personal history to historical social reality. Only weeks later during a therapy session does "Susan" recall and successfully articulate the repressed memory of a childhood rape in a garage, noting that a piñata shaped like a horse hanging from the restaurant ceiling must have triggered the repressed memory of the scene, during which she had dissociated (a form of autohypnosis) by focusing on a child's rocking horse stored in the rafters (Hess 59). In the experience of prolonged trauma, as in cases of repetitive incest or emotional or physical abuse of long duration, repression may be even more severe. The *past reality* of emotional, verbal, and physical violence and neglect is precisely what cannot be spoken, precisely what must be kept hidden within the psychic interiors of the individuated subject, shrouded in a legacy of secrecy, concealment, distortion, and shame. And when it surfaces, if it surfaces at all, it often does so under the sign of mental illness.

The psychopharmacological production of a chemical prosthetic feminine subject recently entered a new mass-culture phase with the newly developed and aggressively marketed serotonin-specific drugs—Desyrel (trazodone), Anafranil (clomipramine), and the trendy and popular Prozac (fluoxetine). Serotonergic systems of the brain interface with the autonomic nervous system. These serotonin-specific drugs suppress hyperarousal and relieve depression by blocking the absorption of excess serotonin in the brain, thus increasing serotonin levels. Billed as the "personality pill" in the June 1993 issue of *Mirabella*, Prozac has been claimed to have wondrous capabilities by the mass media, from making timid introverts socially gregarious and adept, to making businesswomen more productive and self-assured. With fewer side effects than the tricyclic antidepressants (counterindications of Prozac include mild nausea, shakiness, insomnia, and, often downplayed in the promotional literature though commonly reported by users, anorgasmia), Prozac is the

IN ANY SOCIETY BASED ON CLASS, HUMILIATION IS A POLITICAL REALITY. HUMILIATION IS ONE METHOD BY WHICH POLITICAL POWER IS TRANSFORMED INTO SOCIAL OR PERSONAL RELATIONSHIPS. THE PERSONAL INTERIORIZATION OF THE PRACTICE OF HUMILIATION IS CALLED HUMILITY.

—*Kathy Acker*
"Dead Doll Humility"

1990s psychotropic medication for women that has gone mainstream, much like Valium did in the 1960s and 1970s, grossing for Lilly nearly $1 billion of the $8 billion antidepressant revenues for 1992 (Breggin 1994, 3). By 1993, profits rose to $1.2 billion.

While the pharmaceutical industry claims that "personality enhancement" with "cosmetic psychopharmacology" promises to be the great democratizer for people made "vulnerable" by trauma or by innate neural chemistry, psychopharmacology obviously provides a tool for reinforcing cultural norms, reproducing the nervous system's body politic, and channeling abstract-machinic criteria onto real social bodies. The media plays a crucial role in this system of production—a point emphasized by Peter Breggin, M.D., one of the most vocal critics of the biochemical theories of the "New Psychiatry" and of the psychopharmacology industry, or what he terms "the mental health industrial complex" (*Toxic Psychiatry* 1991, *Talking Back to Prozac* 1994). Breggin notes that the great surge in Prozac sales from 1991 to 1994 followed a March 26, 1990, *Newsweek* cover story and the publication of Peter Kramer's *Listening to Prozac* in 1993, which stayed twenty-one weeks on the *New York Times* bestseller list.[14] Not surprisingly, Prozac publicity made its way to women's magazines, such as Elizabeth Stone's article in the June 1993 issue of *Mirabella* titled "The Personality Pill." The article praises Prozac's miraculous accomplishments while taking note of the gender contradictions in Kramer's observation that "women on Prozac often become more active, slightly less attuned to feelings, less concerned about their responsibilities to others. In short, less 'feminine'" (Stone 88).[15]

In terms of channeling the social flow of signs and bodies in the cultural process of becoming-woman in postmodernity, Prozac might well be the successful and ambitious (wo)man's medication of choice, the facilitator of a new hyperthyrmic (if nonorgasmic) definition of feminine normalcy and functionality. A chemical prosthetic democracy proffering "healthy" social functioning even to those social subjects who have suffered economic or social deprivation or traumatic stress from the circulating violences of the nervous system, Prozac promises to be the miracle drug for traumatized and vulnerable populations, a cure for those millions whom Kramer described in the *Mirabella* interview as "people who have suffered serious trauma [who] later find themselves vulnerable to what, for others, would be minor losses or threats of loss" (Stone 92).[16] The postmodern *pharmakon* for social illnesses articulated at the level of individual bodies as, for instance, depression, anxiety, obsessive-compulsive disorder, or bulimia, Prozac already had been prescribed to 6 million Americans and another 4 million people worldwide by 1994 (Rhymer; Breggin, *Talking Back*, 3).

Amid all this neurochemically induced euphoria over cosmetic psychopharmacology, however, the fluctuations of memory (as *surge*) and antimemory (as *suppression*) continue to drive the breakdown of abstract yet concretely embodied feminine subjects while simultaneously structuring their "successful" recovery. In this context, we can't forget that psychopharmacology functions as a modulating mechanism within an abstract-machine materially articulated by psychiatry and psychotherapy for regulating the sign-flux between personal memory and public representations of social history, between public expressions of affect and private memory lacking public validation, and between constructions of (group) desire and the individual's social behavior. Ironically, Kramer himself understands memory to be a determinant of both personality and physiology, and he understands Prozac to alter what he calls the "memory of the body":

And part of what we consider personality—the part corresponding to traumatized monkeys'
reluctance to explore—may be directly encoded by trauma.

A parsimonious, though not entirely comfortable, way of describing these events is to expand our
concept of memory. We readily accept the notion of cognitive and emotional, or at least emotion-
laden, memory. But perhaps sensitivity is memory as well—"the memory of the body,"
as we might say "the wisdom of the body." In this sense, social inhibition and rejection-sensitivity
are both memory. That is, they do not stem from a (cognitive, emotion-laden, conflicted)
memory of trauma; they represent or just are memories of trauma. According to
this way of thinking, much of who Lucy is—her neural pathways, her social needs—
constitutes a biological memory of her mother's murder, just as Tess's social style
is a memory of her precociously responsible childhood. (124)[17]

Nonetheless, Kramer and other proponents of biopsychiatry do not see the alteration of the body's memories as suppression of the history and experiential reality of particular social groups that may have a detrimental effect on the long-term healing process of that group. To what extent, for example, does Tess's "social style" (a virtual masochistic subjection of her own needs and desires to the needs and desires of those around her, accompanied by a high tolerance for inappropriate behavior and recurring depression) constitute the social style of most women who have experienced incest or abuse in childhood (a childhood experience that Kramer in this passage screens as a "precociously responsible childhood")?[18] And what kinds of political action might emerge if Tess connected her lived "body memory" with those who have had similar experiences, rather than rewiring that bodily memory with Prozac?

In fact, psychopharmacological treatments of the nervous system's symptomatologies modulate and channel the social production of the traumatized subject at its point of public manifestation and social organization, reterritorializing its symptomatic (dys)functions as the raw material for techno-industrial capital development and market expansion. Within the general economy of psychopharmacology, the (dys)functional woman is simultaneously the product of a (dys)functional social, the raw material for socioeconomic production, and the consumer market. Within such a political economy of signs, Prozac and all psychotropic medications promise to hold at bay if not "cure" the postmodern subject in its most "normative" form of social expression—that is, as the disordered and dysfunctional subject.

The political stakes are high for current psychiatric practices that channel and modulate the outcomes of deterritorializing desires and of alienated memory and affect, which can express in the public sphere only as dissociation and abreaction (i.e., mental illness). It is doubtful that a "healthy" cultural politics in touch with the historical social reality of the group could ever emerge out of a discourse of recovery as long as "recovery" continues to institutionalize the individuated feminine subject as a screen for the psychopathology of a social body to which she is neither completely exterior nor interior. What (individual's) recovery would be meaningful if the body politic at large remains ill? What would it mean to "recover" from the effects of the nervous system?

From the point of view of *cultural* healing, what the traumatized subject needs is not a chemically induced repressed memory and prosthetic personality, but the reintegration, molecularization, and group expression of her fractal memories and disconnected affects and desires, not only within the private sphere of her own individual psyche and in her direct relations to the institutional workings of the nervous system, but within the public sphere of collective representations of embodied social reality. Accomplishing such a molecular politics would require of the traumatized feminine subject not only the ability to remember and articulate publicly violence's past and her role in that past but also the capacity to forget—not as an act of repression, but as a conscious act of deterritorializing the politics of desire and the social process of subjectification at the micropolitical level of her own memories, emotions, and desires. Whether or not she uses psychotropic chemical treatments to do so is not the issue.[19] The issue is whether the psychopharmacological machine is channeling her or whether she in some way is channeling it toward a historically informed collective notion of what would constitute a meaningful social response to being subject to, and becoming-woman within, postmodern culture's agitated nervous system.

IN A DREAM YOU SAW A WAY TO SURVIVE AND YOU WERE FULL OF JOY

—Jenny Holzer "Survival," from *The Venice Installation*

Notes

Preface

1. Editorial, "Femme Fatale," *New York Times*, February 2, 1991, A-22.

2. Hyman Rodman, Betty Sarvis, and Joy Bonar, *The Abortion Question*. New York: Columbia University Press, 1987.

3. Ironically, Linda Bray and her unit were later investigated by the military for their conduct under fire during the U.S. invasion of Panama. Though the investigation turned up no proof of misconduct, she was separated from her unit and, in her words, "harassed" for the media attention she attracted. Peter Copeland, "As Battle Ended Burden Began for Celebrated Woman Warrior," *Rocky Mountain News*, June 30, 1991, 4.

4. There are no comprehensive statistics on who uses Prozac, but doctors and the manufacturer Eli Lilly agree the majority are women between the ages of twenty and fifty. Sara Rimer, "With Millions Taking Prozac, a Legal Drug Culture Arises," *New York Times*, December 13, 1993, S-1.

5. Gina Kolata, "Breast Implant Companies Dispute Claim of Settlement," *New York Times*, March 19, 1994, A-8.

6. The New York State Department of Health estimated 4,000 surrogate births in 1992 at a cost of $33 million to contracting couples. Lisa Belkin, "Surrogate Laws vs. Last Hope of the Childless: Facing New Restrictions in New York Couples Vow to Find Loopholes," *New York Times*, July 18, 1992, B-1.

7. Judith Brady, ed., *1 in 3: Women with Cancer Confront an Epidemic*. Pittsburgh: Cleis Press, 1991.

8. Eli Lilly enjoyed a 30 percent growth in Prozac profits in 1993 from the previous year. Timothy Egan, "A Washington City Full of Prozac," *New York Times*, January 30, 1994, 1, 16.

9. On the distinction between the virtual and the possible, the actual and the real, in Deleuze's work, Hardt writes: "Deleuze asserts that it is essential that we conceive of the Bergsonian emanation of being, differentiation, as a relationship between the *virtual* and the *actual*, rather than as a relationship between the *possible* and the *real*. After setting up these two couples (virtual-actual and possible-real), Deleuze proceeds to note that the transcendental term of each couple relates positively to the immanent term of the opposite couple. The possible is never real, even though it may be actual; however, while the virtual may not be actual, it is nonetheless real. In other words, there are several contemporary (actual) possibilities of which some may be realized in the future; in contrast, virtualities are always real (in the past, in memory) and may become actualized in the present" (1993, 16–17).

10. See Braidotti's essay "Feminist Deleuzian Tracks; or, Metaphysics and Metabolism" and Grosz's essay "A

Thousand Tiny Sexes: Feminism and Rhizomatics" in *Gilles Deleuze and the Theater of Philosophy*, ed. Boundas and Olkowski (1994).

11. Hardt notes in his reading of the early Deleuze that the philosophical concept of "becoming" is posed in opposition to "the dialectical unity of the One and the Multiple." The concept of becoming is born from a materialist ontology in which practice, not thought, is constitutive of being (xiv).

1. The Despotic Face of White Femininity

1. Harlow's research suggested that the simulation of ears, eyes, mouth, and nostrils was more significant to human researchers than to monkey infants in the construction of the surrogate. This finding points to the structural foundation of faciality as a machinic assemblage that begins with the constitution of a space in which the percept can appear. In this regard, the cage (not figured in this photograph) is as much a part of the surrogate "face" as the wire and cloth body. Faciality as a signifying and subjectifying system can only emanate from within a constituted screenal space. Constituting a screenal space is the first function of faciality as an abstract-machine that translates the organic, proprioceptive body-head system into a technological face system.

2. See Donna Haraway's discussion of Harlow's hypothesis that "maternal rejection" caused psychopathology (not the experiments themselves) in "Metaphors into Hardware: Harlow and the Technology of Love" (*Primate Visions*, 238). Haraway notes about individual monkeys separated from their mothers early after birth who were kept isolated in cages: "These animals showed gross behavioral trouble, staring into space, clutching themselves and performing unending stereotypic automatic movements" (238).

3. Biunivocalization places constraint on the proliferation of sexualities: "Sexuality is the production of a thousand sexes, which are so many uncontrollable becomings. Sexuality proceeds by way of the becoming-woman of the man and the becoming-animal of the human: an emission of particles" (Deleuze 1987, 278).

4. I take the term "despotic" from Massumi's translation of Deleuze and Guattari in *A Thousand Plateaus* (1987). The imperial despotic regime of signs is ruled by the signifier. It has eight aspects: (1) signs that refer to other signs ad infinitum; (2) circularity in the process of deterritorialization of signs; (3) "hysterical" jumping of the sign from one layer of circularity to another while maintaining the center; (4) the regulation of interpretations that "reimpart the signifier" so as to guarantee the expansion of the circles; (5) a supreme signifier presenting as "both lack and excess" and generating an infinite set of signs; (6) the despotic

signifier having both a form and substance; (7) any line of flight from the despotic regime of signs being assigned a negative value and condemned; (8) the regime works by deception in all its aspects (1987, 117). In this regard, biunivocalization is a mechanism of despotic imperialism: "Whatever the differences between signifiance and subjectification, whichever prevails over the other in this case or that, whatever the varying figures assumed by their de facto mixtures—they have it in common to crush all polyvocality, set up language as a form of exclusive expression, and operate by signifying biunivocalization and subjective binarization" (1987, 180).

5. On the distinctions among territorialization, deterritorialization, and reterritorialization, Deleuze and Guattari write that territorialization "reorganizes functions" and "regroups forces" within supple, segmentary social space (so-called tribal space) (1987, 320), while reterritorialization, which implies the specific striating procedures of a state apparatus, "is not an added territory, but takes place in a different space than that of territories, namely, overcoded geometrical space." Likewise, "overcoding is not a stronger code, but a specific procedure different from that of codes" (1987, 222). The striations of the state are in turn subject to decoding and deterritorializing processes, lines of flight on which "there is always something like a *war machine* functioning." These relations are not linear but rhizomatic: "In truth, codes are never separable from the movement of decoding, nor are territories from the vectors of deterritorialization traversing them. And overcoding and reterritorialization do not come after. It would be more accurate to say that there is a space in which the three kinds of closely intermingled lines coexist, tribes, empires, and war machines" (222).

6. Unlike *Vogue* and *Harper's Bazaar*, *Elle* has no formal permissions office. My request for permission to reproduce the cover of the June 1991 issue was channeled to marketing, and from there to Jean Fornasieri, associate editor of *Elle*. Treating my academic request as an issue of marketing and advertising rather than scholarship and education, she declined permission for the cover to appear in this text because she didn't feel it appropriately represented the magazine's interests. The cover features two models in profile, one white, one of color, but both wearing identical clothing and accessories and sporting the same haircut. Interestingly, the clothing company Kikit also refused permission to reproduce an ad in which two female models are kissing. I could not help but wonder if the term "lesbian chic" was what was causing these advertisers to act so manifestly despotically in regard to the signifier. Thus, the two images of lesbian chic that were to appear in this book are absent.

7. On the function of the white man's face as a translating machine in racism, Deleuze and Guattari write: "Racism operates by the determination of degrees of deviance in relation to the White-Man face, which endeavors to integrate nonconforming traits into increasingly eccentric and backward waves, sometimes tolerating them at given places under given conditions, in a given ghetto, sometimes erasing them from the wall, which never abides alterity (it's a Jew, it's an Arab, it's a Negro, it's a lunatic . . .). From the viewpoint of racism, there is no exterior, there are no people on the outside" (1987, 178).

8. Japanese newsreel footage of Nagasaki and Hiroshima immediately after the atomic bombings was confiscated by the U.S. government and censored as classified material until 1970. See Barnouw on the production history of the film *Hiroshima-Nagasaki, August 1945*, which was made from documentary and newsreel footage of the A-bombs' aftermath, released in the United States in 1970.

9. At thirteen, Isabella Rossellini's scoliosis was treated with orthopedic surgery and a plaster body cast. In an article about her in the *New York Times* after *Blue Velvet*'s release, she reported that she used the memory of the pain from the surgery that corrected her corporeal flaws as inspiration for her acting. See Laurie Winer, "Isabella Rossellini Assesses the Role That Haunted Her," *New York Times*, November 23, 1986, A-21.

10. Benetton advertisements, featuring Haitian refugees, for example, have to some extent deterritorialized this limit-face of the sacrifice in advertising. Still a rarity in the general landscape of advertising, however, such ads produce a tremendous amount of shock value. While they make visible what is usually invisible, they nonetheless continue to locate the sacrifice under the sign of difference (Haitians, a young man dying of AIDS) rather than sameness (i.e., the woman next door who's a victim of domestic violence, or children of any U.S. inner-city ghetto). In this regard, Benetton ads, while seeming to rupture the surface screen of the despotic signifier, nonetheless continue to contain the sacrifice as that which is "without" and "other." Ironically, the appearance of a Benetton store in urban renewal projects in the United States usually signifies advanced gentrification in a process in which local minorities are displaced by upwardly mobile baby boomer yuppies.

11. On the relation of subjectivization to the authoritarian assemblage, Deleuze and Guattari write: "There is more to the picture than semiotic systems waging war on one another armed only with their own weapons. Very specific assemblages of power impose signiance and subjectification as their determinate form of expression, in reciprocal presupposition with new contents: there is no signiance without a despotic assemblage, no subjectification without an authoritarian assemblage, and no mixture between the two without assemblages of power that act through signifiers and act upon souls and subjects. It is these assemblages, these

despotic or authoritarian formations, that give the new semiotic system the means of its imperialism, in other words, the means to crush the other semiotics and protect itself against any threat from outside" (1987, 81).

12. Bob Guccione of *Penthouse* specified that I could reproduce an image from *Penthouse Variations* only if I used the word *erotica* rather than *pornography* in my text. After some discussion with *Penthouse* representatives and with press editors, I attempted to comply with this request in order to reproduce the image. I see their insistence as another instance of academic signification being reterritorialized by the commodified signifier. My revision, however, did not satisfy Mr. Guccione and permission was denied.

13. On the grammatical function of the face, Deleuze and Guattari write: "A language is always embedded in the faces that announce its statements and ballast them in relation to the signifiers in progress and subjects concerned. Choices are guided by faces, elements are organized around faces: a common grammar is never separable from a facial education. The face is a veritable megaphone" (1987, 179). Erotic images fetishize and commodify the desire of the undisciplined tongue to rupture grammatical faciality.

14. *Penthouse Variations* ran an ad in its March 1995 issue showing a television monitor in which the letters "COMING INTERACTIVE SEX ON TV" were projected onto the back of a woman's naked torso. The ad campaign previews the coming face of femininity as the erotica industry and the interactive telecommunications industry merge.

15. Deleuze and Guattari write on the relation of the organic to subjectification and signiance: "A concerted effort is made to do away with the body and corporeal coordinates through which the multidimensional or polyvocal semiotics operated. Bodies are disciplined, corporeality dismantled, becomings-animal hounded out, deterritorialization pushed to a new threshold—a jump is made from the organic strata to the strata of signiance and subjectification" (1987, 181).

16. After a performance at the Virtual Futures Conference at the University of Warwick in May 1995 (in which one young woman in the audience fainted), Orlan discussed the difference between the abjection she hopes to stir in her art and the sadness one feels for the women who feel they must alter their faces out of dissatisfaction and social pressure to conform to cultural norms.

17. See Avital Ronell's *The Telephone Book: Technology, Schizophrenia, Electric Speech* for an extended discussion of the modern desire to reterritorialize maternal functions within technological functions.

18. Compare, for example, Crone's *Chemicals and Society: A Guide to the New Chemical Age* with Brady's *1 in 3:*

Women with Cancer Confront an Epidemic. The former is written by a biochemist and researcher, the latter written by a collective of women who are writers or self-taught activists, all of whom have or have had cancer. One of Crone's arguments is that the increase in cancer rates is due primarily to the fact that people are living longer (thanks to the chemical control of infections) (85). This argument, however, downplays the significance of statistical studies of cancer that are age-standardized, in which the cancer rate of one age group (say per 100,000 people) at one time is compared with the rate of that same age group (per 100,000) at later times. For example, when the rate of testicular cancer for men ages 25–34 in 1950 is compared to that of men in the same age group in 1988, the data show about a 300 percent increase (Cancer Statistics Review). Based on the findings of such studies, longer life expectancy cannot account for the escalating increase in overall cancers (Epstein 17–19).

19. *The Merck Index, 11th Edition.* Rahway, N.J.: Merck, 1989. Dioxin (1436), hexachlorobenzene (740), PCBS (1204).

20. With the total rate of cancer 1 in 3 (Brady, Epstein).

21. I will note, however, that the language of the marketplace, mapped onto tropes of gender, is deeply embedded in medical discourse on reconstructive breast surgery. Neal Handel, a plastic surgeon from The Breast Cancer Center in Van Nuys, California, wrote in his article on "state of the art" breast reconstruction techniques: "Breast reconstruction after mastectomy can make an important contribution to the quality of life of women with breast cancer. Reconstruction eliminates the need for a cumbersome external prosthesis, allows greater freedom in the selection of clothing styles, and makes a woman more comfortable undressing in front of others. Reconstruction also reduces anxiety and depression and helps a woman regain a sense of wholeness and femininity" (Handel 73). This rhetoric assumes that the mastectomy should be covered up and that the breast is an essential organ of femininity.

2. Lesbian Bodies in the Age of (Post)mechanical Reproduction

1. I am using the term "postmodern culture" in reference specifically to Lyotard's usage in *The Postmodern Condition*—that is, as a reference to a level of incredulity toward the master narratives of modernization, technologization, and progress (not as a reference to the failure of any of these master narratives, per se).

2. Jan van Eyck's "Giovanni Arnolfini and His Bride" (1434) is a notable secular variation in which the pregnant woman can enter representation, but only under the category of property. The Demi Moore cover may make reference to this famous icon as well.

3. Bright got pregnant "the old-fashioned way"—"I lay on a water bed with a real live man, someone whose genes and fatherly temperament I've been admiring for some time"—a fact that she made public in the closing chapter of her first book, *Susie Sexpert's Lesbian Sex World* (1990).

4. See Califia's early work with SAMOIS.

5. Photographic and electronic imaging media— including photo-journals, popular film, broadcast and cable TV, home video and on-line transmissions—have mainstreamed lesbian images by disseminating them to broadcast audiences. The popular controversy over Madonna's *Justify Your Love* music video, which appeared late in 1990, exemplifies the continual process of semiotic assimilation. In this postmodern conundrum, Madonna not only *becomes lesbian* for a portion of the tape, but the lesbian subtext becomes, if not MTV, then broadcast news—specifically, ABC's *Nightline*, which aired the video in its entirety to millions of late-night television viewers. *Elle*'s butch-femme aesthetic—which has managed not to "go too far" as Madonna's video did—is successfully becoming majority fashion-feminine for a growing segment of the middle-class and upper-middle-class women's market. *L.A. Law*, meanwhile, is mainstreaming for prime-time soap audiences the everyday aporias of how to comport oneself with, as, and for a lesbian. *Thelma and Louise*, making the cover of *Time* the summer of its release with a photograph of Susan Sarandon and Geena Davis looking both butch *and* exactly like each other under the heading "Why *Thelma and Louise* Strikes a Nerve" (June 24, 1991), is just another event in a long series of discursive assimilations that are producing the popular cultural generation of the new butch-femme. Lesbians are out, and they are "passing" as versions of normative femininity.

6. The dis-organ-ized body, in Deleuze and Guattari's (1987) micromental study of capitalism and schizophrenia, is the Body without Organs (BwO).

7. See Sandy Stone's account and critique of the "gender dysphoria syndrome" in "The Empire Strikes Back: A Posttranssexual Manifesto" in *Body Guards*.

8. Rhizomatic principles include connection, heterogeneity, multiplicity, segmentarity (asignifying rupture), cartography, and decalcomania. Each principle is discussed in the introduction to *A Thousand Plateaus*. On the relation of the book to rhizomatic thought, Deleuze and Guattari write: "One becomes two: whenever we encounter this formula, even stated strategically by Mao or understood in the most 'dialectical' way possible, what we have before us is the most classical and well reflected, oldest, and weariest kind of thought. Nature doesn't work that way: in nature, roots are taproots with a more multiple, lateral, and circular system of ramification, rather than a dichotomous one. Thought lags behind nature. Even the book as a natural reality is a taproot, with its pivotal spine and surrounding leaves" (1987, 5).

For Deleuze and Guattari, everything is at stake in getting beyond biunivocalization: "Binary logic and biunivocal relationships still dominate psychoanalysis (the tree of delusion in the Freudian interpretation of Schreber's case), linguistics, structuralism, and even information science" (5).

9. According to Ong, mechanical production began with the reification of the oral world/word into print. Typography "literally" made the word into a commodity (*Orality* 119, 131).

10. Benjamin's discourse comes close to a discourse of degenerescence and decadence anchored in a notion of the "natural" when he reads mechanical reproduction as a process of cultural "liquidation," and when he approaches the historical object as if it were analogous to the aura of the "natural" object. He's reluctant to let go of the modern notion of history as composed of objects bearing the same permanence and value as nature, and for good reason—fascism was obviously in its pragmatics a project of rewriting history. This is the contradiction of any nationalist totalitarian regime of signs: it fetishizes technology at the very time that it mobilizes nostalgic traces of a romantic notion of a "natural" socius. Perhaps Benjamin couldn't bring himself to say that the "authority" of the traditional cultural heritage that he appeals to in the face of fascism is itself purely constructed—depending on its own class structures and techniques of representation for reproduction and enforcement. The (constructed) authority of this "original" heritage in the minds of the masses would be appropriated more easily than anyone could have imagined by fascist dream machines using the new technologies of mass reproduction, epitomized in the Nazis' use of broadcast radio and the newsreel—media that Benjamin correctly recognized as new forms of armaments (213). The Nazis' genocidal program demonstrated that history *could* be rewritten, in a matter of a few years, and that the "real" history that purportedly would have saved the world from the kind of contorted fantasy of national history and identity that Hitler cathected had no *essential* authority whatsoever. Fascism, in fact, proceeds as a possibility from the very moment that the masses come to perceive themselves as the technologized subject of nature, and no longer as object of nature.

11. The legal implications of this scenario await testing in regard to the law recognizing both the biological mother and birth mother as legal parents bearing full rights. I'm assuming in the scenario an artificial insemination by anonymous donor.

12. The more this process of becoming minoritarian occurs, however, (and, of course, it's always occurring),

the more difficult it becomes for the majoritarian body to "resist infiltration," and the more necessary it becomes for dominant straight culture ("traditional values" coalitions, etc.) to protect all borders fronting on otherness. "Resisting infiltration" suggests a paranoid posture—one that denies the constant process of psychic auto-organization and reorganization—a process made visible particularly by subcultural collective identities organized around the erotic cultivation of the intersubjective transactions and psychic instabilities common to amatory relations. For this reason, Kristeva (1987) describes the amorous relations as a *vertigo of identity*. Rather than return the gaze of a body functioning manifestly as a collapsed inside/outside system in interaction with a multidimensional and fluid (i.e., excessive, unnatural, monstrous) psychic system, the paranoid will take flight to a prolapsed symbolic, thereby stabilizing the illusion of an identity as a stable relation to a fixed sign formation (i.e., a natural signatory relation of "self" to others).

13. See Wittig's argument for a lesbian total subject in "The Mark of Gender," for example (1992).

14. John D'Emilio, in *Sexual Politics, Sexual Communities*, describes the historical context in which "same-sex eroticism" emerges in the United States as an assemblage of factors: "On the one hand, cumulative historical processes—spread of capitalist economic relations, industrialism, and the socialization of production, and urban growth—were shaping a social context in which homosexual desire might congeal into a personal identity" (22). On military recruitment of single women during World War II, see *Total War* (Willis 1991), particularly the chapter "Substitute Bodies."

15. The 1970s women's movement and the 1960s African American civil rights movement shared similar ties to the war machine, through the substitute bodies recruitment policy in U.S. universities during World War II and through the GI Bill.

16. See Creet's "Daughter of the Movement: The Psychodynamics of Lesbian S/M Fantasy" on the political tension between gay-identified S/M lesbians and maternally identified feminists.

3. Becoming War-Machine

1. On the distinction between *assemblage* and *machine*, Deleuze and Guattari write: "Whenever a territorial assemblage is taken up by a movement that deterritorializes it (whether under so-called natural or artificial conditions), we say that a machine is released. That in fact is the distinction we would like to propose between machine and assemblage: a machine is like a set of cutting edges that insert themselves into the assemblage undergoing deterritorialization, and draw variations and mutations of it.... What we call machinic statements are machine effects that define consistency or enter matters of expression. Effects of this kind can be very diverse but are never symbolic or imaginary; they always have a real value of passage or relay" (333).

2. See Cynthia Enloe's "Base Women" in her *Bananas, Beaches, Bases: Making Feminist Sense of International Politics* on the role of military wives in the reproduction of military-base life (72).

3. De Landa goes on to state an example from biochemistry: "A well-known example is the chemical reaction known as Belousov-Zhabotinsy, where the random interaction of billions of molecules leads to the self-assembly of a chemical clock. That is, in certain special conditions the molecules in the reaction can self-organize and begin pulsating to a perfect beat. Because this spontaneous generation of order seemed to contradict well-established principles of science, self-assembled chemical clocks remained for a long time outside the bounds of science, regarded at most as interesting anomalies, curiosities to be explained away. However, in the last thirty years (thanks in part to the extensive use of computers as tools for exploration) a new physics and a new mathematics have taken shape, and the old anomalies have come to be seen as representing a fundamental property of matter-energy. Examples of self-organizing phenomena have now been discovered in many different fields (hydrodynamics, biology, economics, cognitive science) and the whole enterprise is now experiencing an explosive growth" (1992, 127).

4. On the relation of human technology to the machinic phylum, De Landa states: "Defined in this way, it should be obvious that the machinic phylum relates to human technology only in a secondary sense. For example, it first and foremost addresses the question of the self-assembly of hurricanes, which are steam engines in a very literal sense, and only in a derivative way to the human assembly of steam-motors in the eighteenth century. So in this sense, it is not 'the model of the machine' that occupies the place of the sacred in my work" (1992, 129).

5. See De Landa's "Policing the Spectrum" in *War in the Age of Intelligent Machines.*

6. France provides a model of military recruitment and regulation of women within an active conscription system. In the French military in 1991, women were 1.6 percent of commissioned officers, 1.8 percent of junior enlisted personnel, but 8.3 percent of noncommissioned officers. The flow of women into the French armed services as noncommissioned officers is constrained by annual recruitment quotas at 8 percent of the total NCO corps (Boulègue).

7. Policy changes removing restrictions on assigning women to combat positions may change this configuration in the future. In the National Defense Authorization Act for Fiscal Years 1992 and 1993, Public Law 102–190 — December 5, 1991, Congress amended language in 10 U.S.C. 6015 relating to the assignment of women in the Navy and Marine Corps and repealed 10 U.S.C. 8549, which restricted the Air Force's assignment of women (*Women in Combat: Report to the President*, B-1).

8. Department of Defense funding practices in higher education were established during World War I and World War II, when depleted student bodies suffered by wartime universities were compensated for by military or "national service" training programs. In 1945, Department of Defense programs and grants were contributing as much as 50 percent of the income of some universities and colleges. These funding practices, which continued after wartime, favored technical and professional courses considered useful to a war effort, such as communications, engineering, management, petroleum geology, and medicine (Willis 75–78). The effects of defense-funded training programs on universities caused Senator Fulbright to state during the Vietnam War that U.S. universities had "betrayed a public trust when they became dependent on government-sponsored research projects" (Arendt 16).

9. In late November 1992, while the popular press was busily mediating the controversy over then president-elect Clinton's campaign promise to end, by presidential order if necessary, the forty-eight-year-old military policy of discharging gays and lesbians, the Naval Reserve Officers Training Corps (ROTC) was ordering student enlistees to sign affadavits acknowledging that they were not gay and that they would be expelled from the program and forced to return scholarship money if later found to be gay (Chibbaro). Such policies obviously closeted many more gay and lesbian enlistees, whose bodies the military could hardly do without, than they actually expelled. Clinton's "compromise" agreement with the Pentagon over lifting the ban, described by the media as "Don't ask; don't tell," does at least outlaw this type of official surveillance policy.

10. Or other forms of popular representation, such as the mainstreaming of virtual reality military training programs. I had the opportunity to try out one virtual reality proto-arcade game that has recently been circulating on university campuses, variations of which one would expect will soon enough be targeted for arcade malls. In this three-dimensional reality simulator, two competitive players attempt to shoot each other while monitoring potential attacks from the air — an obvious spin-off of military training technologies. A "feminine" subject position is "virtually" nonexistent in the playing field. Female participation in the game, like male participation, requires identification with a masculine, predatory, virtual persona. The gender and depredations of that persona are inscribed in the visual icon of a man who moves in the playing field and who can be seen by the opponent, and in the channeling of each player's agency into a "move forward" and "fire" option on a hand-control fashioned in the shape of a gun. (I could hear my "opponent," who happened to be one of my graduate students, being coached by an audience observing the game on video monitors: "*He's* to your left; shoot *him*!"). The "flight or fight" adrenal network of the lower brain stem is stimulated by the interiorized sound of a pulsating heartbeat pumped through a (male) opponent. The point is that the game requires the contribution of human players as necessary components to operate; nonetheless, these players direct the machinically organized game far less than the game plays and directs the players once they have entered the playing field—a simulated space that exists only as a result of the Defense Department's Advanced Research Programs Agency tracking the calculating and digital imaging capabilities of computers and video.

11. This would be a variation on the panopticon that Foucault theorizes in *Discipline and Punish*, in which the surveillance system has become simultaneously exteriorized and interiorized through the media.

12. Not only are women always potential civilian victims in contemporary warfare, but they are also primary caretakers for the victims of war who survive. Consider, for example, the plight of mothers of children born to Gulf War veterans who suffer from "Gulf War syndrome." According to a 1994 report by the General Accounting Office, "American soldiers were exposed to 21 potential 'reproductive toxicants,' any of which might have harmed [servicemen and civilian support technicians] and their future children" (Briggs and Miller 52). Toxicants during the Gulf War included diesel fuel used to keep down sand, smoke from burning oil wells, pesticides, shells tipped with depleted uranium, a nerve-gas decontaminant (ethylene glycol monomethyl ether), and PB (pyridostigmine bromide), an experimental drug that was given to most Americans in the Gulf as a pretreatment for nerve gas. The children of some of these veterans suffer horrific birth defects reminiscent of Agent Orange and thalidomide.

13. See "1227: Treatise on Nomadology: The War Machine" in *A Thousand Plateaus* on the distinction between nomadic smooth space and the striated space of the state—between the nomadic war machine and the state's always incomplete and unsuccessful project to appropriate it as its own in the form of a state-appropriated war machine (351). Deleuze and Guattari write: "There are many reasons to believe that the war machine is of a different origin, is a different assemblage, than the State apparatus. It is of nomadic origin and is directed against the State apparatus. One of the fundamental problems of the State is to appropriate this war machine that is foreign to it and make it a piece in its apparatus, in the form of a stable military institution; and the State has always encountered major difficulties in

this. It is precisely when the war machine has reached the point that it has no other object but war, it is when it substitutes destruction for mutation, that it frees the most catastrophic charge. Mutation is in no way a transformation of war; on the contrary, war is like the fall or failure of mutation, the only object left for the war machine after it has lost its power to change" (230). The complexity of the relations between nomadic war machine and the State are exemplified in the debates on the stirrup: "The problem is that it is generally difficult to distinguish between what comes from the nomads as such, and what they receive from the empire they communicate with, conquer, or integrate with" (404).

4. "Feticidal" Attractors

1. The concept of the "material" in Deleuze and Guattari's work includes a potentiality that may or may not be harnessed at any given moment; the material bears a potentiality that may be virtual or actual, depending upon current forces engaged in a given assemblage: "Material thus has three principal characteristics: it is a molecularized matter; it has a relation to forces to be harnessed; and it is defined by the operations of consistency applied to it" (1987, 345).

2. Japan's legalization of abortion depends in no way on this claim to the woman's constitutional right to "individual bodily autonomy" (hardly surprising in Japan, where the linguistic sign for individual identity was imported from the French). This marked difference suggests the distinct ideological reification at work in U.S. cultural discourses rationalizing the "abortion" debate (Tribe 60–65).

3. In 1994, 1.1 percent of births in Japan were to unwed mothers, compared to 30.1 percent in the United States (*New York Times*, March 13, 1996, A1).

5. Lesbians and the Serial Killing-Machine

1. The issue here is, again, one of (im)perceptibility. Which violences are "visible," that is, intelligible to the public? And which remain manifest and yet "unnameable" as violence as such? The media regulate these distinctions. Wuornos can sign in the public sphere as the agent of violence, but not as the recipient; thus her plea to the charge of serial killing—guilty ("I did it") but innocent ("I acted in self-defense")—remained to the public at large a completely incomprehensible statement. Her assemblage of signs, however, clearly exceeds the semiotic register of "serial killing" established in previous usage. Imagine Ted Bundy, Son of Sam, or the Boston Strangler pleading "self-defense."

6. Breakdown

1. Deleuze and Guattari define "affect" precisely as that which exceeds the individuated self: "For the affect is not a personal feeling, nor is it a characteristic; it is the effectuation of a power of the pack that throws the self into upheaval and makes it reel" (1987, 240).

2. Abstract-machines in Deleuze and Guattari's usage both rigidly overcode and decode/mutate: "In view of this, it would be better to talk about simultaneous states of the abstract machine. There is on the one hand an abstract machine of overcoding: it defines a rigid segmentarity, a macrosegmentarity, because it produces or rather reproduces segments, opposing them two by two, making all the centers resonate, and laying out a divisible, homogeneous space striated in all directions. This kind of abstract machine is linked to the State apparatus. . . . On the other hand, at the other pole, there is an abstract machine of mutation, which operates by decoding and deterritorialization. It is what draws the lines of flight; it steers the quantum flows, assures the connection-creation of flows, and emits new quanta" (1987, 223).

3. See Taussig's work on terror's system of production in *Shamanism, Colonialism, and the Wildman* (1987) and *The Nervous System* (1992).

4. After her battle with the research institution, once Genie was turned over to the state of California's foster home program, Genie's files report a period of language shutdown accompanied by severe constipation — resulting at one point in a foster "mother" extracting fecal matter forcibly with a kitchen utensil (Rhymer).

5. The dispute between Genie's teacher, Jean Butler, and the funded academic researcher Susan Curtiss over Genie's capacity to use language was long-standing. Curtiss, who published her dissertation on Genie's language acquisition, concluded from her research that Genie could articulate only through her right brain. Electronic neurological testing showed Genie's left brain, the site of linguistic syntax and grammar, to be physically intact yet completely dysfunctional when Genie spoke. Curtiss concluded that this aspect of neurolinguistic function could never be reactivated. Butler (later Jean Butler Ruch) maintained until her death, however, that Genie would sit and chat with her while she was staying in her home, and that the presence of researchers and environmental stressors caused Genie to shut down. A journal entry during Genie's stay comments: "I asked Dr. Kent to have Miss Curtiss removed from my home, as she was no help but completely untrained and inexperienced with children and had no awareness of safety factors. Dr. Kent said it was necessary to have her here and the need for phonetic recording of speech attempts was more important than her lack of ability in helping with Genie. I pointed out that Genie did not talk around Miss Curtiss" (Rhymer 99). David Freedman, a professor of psychiatry at Baylor College of Medicine, supported Butler's view that Genie's language acquisition and language use were emotional-state dependent, and that what Genie needed

was educational assistance in an emotionally safe environment: " 'I believe a necessary precursor to any effective educative process would be her development of an intense, dependent attachment to some one person whom she would be interested both in identifying herself with and in pleasing . . . ' " (60). While Curtiss would not remove herself from Genie's potential healing space with Jean Butler, nor agree that Genie's language skills were dependent upon her affective state, she had no problem admitting the severity of Genie's trauma: " 'Being with Genie wasn't like being with a retarded person. It was like being with a disturbed person. She was the most disturbed person I'd ever met' " (127). Interestingly, Curtiss also admitted that Genie could communicate nonverbally — though this phenomenon was not subjected to scientific research. Apparently, when Genie went out in the world, strangers would stop in the street, women and children mostly, to hand over objects to her (93). Children would silently hand over their toys. A woman stopped at a red light, emptied out her purse on the floorboard, handed it to Genie, ran back to her car, and drove off. Did these people share some unspeakable knowledge that made Genie's "unspoken" language (her faciality and gestures) familiar and intelligible? The point is that Genie's language organ was not "missing" but simply deterritorialized from her mouth and rearticulated by her desiring-machine across her other organs, including apparently her eyes as well as her entire body's spatial relation to objects. Rhymer's account is full of different people's descriptions of this aspect of Genie's being.

6. David and Marilyn Rigler presented a symposium paper on Genie's phobic response to the household dog entitled "Attenuation of Severe Phobia in a Historic Case of Extreme Psychosocial Deprivation" at the Twentieth International Congress of Psychology (Rhymer 141).

7. Only Jean Butler read Genie's "missing language organ" as a sign of Genie's volition, that is, her choice to shut down and her refusal to make social connections she did not desire.

8. The media participates in a similar economy at the level of mass culture by channeling repressed memories of everyday terror into either sensationalized news events of a few seconds' duration or made-for-TV evening movies about incest or domestic abuse, replete with commercial breaks. Avant-garde art, literature, and film work on the same cultural plane — screening the unrepresentable — though tackling it at the level of codes of apperception (for a much smaller audience).

9. Mass-mediating and politicizing "acting out" behavior within the public sphere is the basis of ACT-UP politics.

10. On the "abnormal," Deleuze and Guattari comment: "It has been noted that the origin of the word anomal ('anomalous'), an adjective that has fallen into disuse in

French, is very different from that of anormal ('abnormal'): a-normal, a Latin adjective lacking a noun in French, refers to that which is outside rules or goes against the rules, whereas an-omalie, a Greek noun that has lost its adjective, designates the unequal, the coarse, the rough, the cutting edge of deterritorialization. The abnormal can be defined only in terms of characteristics, specific or generic; but the anomalous is a position or set of positions in relation to a multiplicity. Sorcerers therefore use the old adjective 'anomalous' to situate the positions of the exceptional individual to the pack" (1987, 244).

11. Kramer is commenting on Tess — his most remarkable "makeover" case of Prozac treatment, in an interview with *Mirabella* magazine in 1993 (Stone). Tess's case study lies at the heart of Kramer's argument for cosmetic psychopharmacology in *Listening to Prozac*; his account of her case opens the book.

12. Analysis of the sociohistorical structures of power relating abstract forms and collective social contents at a multitude of micropolitical levels is the heart of Félix Guattari's revisionist psychoanalysis and the crux of his political critique of the psychiatric institution in *Molecular Revolution: Psychiatry and Politics* (1984).

13. Deleuze and Guattari discuss the semiotic and social function of silence through the figure of the "Secret": "The secret as content is superseded by a perception of the secret, which is no less secret than the secret. It matters little what the goal is, and whether the aim of the perception is a denunciation, final divulging, or disclosure. From an anecdotal standpoint, the perception of the secret is the opposite of the secret, but from the standpoint of the concept, it is a part of it. What counts is that the perception of the secret must necessarily be secret itself" (1987, 287).

14. Kramer became a celebrity during the media's love affair with Prozac, landing him in a number of featured interviews. Kramer describes his climb to notoriety in the introduction to his book: "I write a monthly column in a trade paper for psychiatrists, and in it I began musing aloud about Prozac. First I wrote about Sam and his sense that medication simultaneously transformed him and taught him how he was put together. Then I wrote about patients who became 'better than well,' patients who acquired extra energy and became socially attractive. My mnemonic for this effect was 'cosmetic psychopharmacology.' That two word phrase, as it happened, did for me what Prozac had done for certain of my patients: it made me instantly popular. By the time my second essay about Prozac appeared, in March 1990, the drug was hot. It had appeared on the cover of *New York Magazine* and was about to hit the national media. I was the psychiatrist who had written about Prozac — I had said out loud what thousands of doctors had observed — and as a result, I was due my fifteen minutes in the limelight. I was quoted in a cover story in

Newsweek, interviewed on talk radio, asked for opinions by any number of magazine and newspaper reporters, and finally referenced in the definitive contemporary article for physicians on the use of antidepressants, in the *New England Journal of Medicine*" (xvi).

In contrast, Peter R. Breggin's critique of the psychopharmacology industry, *Toxic Psychiatry: Why Therapy, Empathy and Love Must Replace the Drugs, Electroshock and Biochemical Theories of the New Psychiatry* (St. Martin's Press, 1991), was reviewed by only one major U.S. paper, the *San Francisco Chronicle*, even though the book sold 30,000 copies (Breggin, "Prozac Talks," 15).

15. In *Listening to Prozac*, Kramer writes: "Prozac highlights our culture's preference for certain personality types. Vivacious women's attractiveness to men, the contemporary scorn of fastidiousness, men's discomfort with anhedonia [the inability to experience pleasure] in women, the business advantage conferred by mental quickness — all these examples point to a consistent social prejudice" (270).

16. In his book, Kramer also describes a "reactive" person susceptible to dysthymia, for whom "what might seem to others quite minor stress will be experienced as trauma," suggesting a cofactor model of depression determined by "traumatic events in the life history of someone with a vulnerable temperamental predisposition" (192).

17. One should note that this recognition of a "memory of the body" is the basis for a variety of alternative, nonpsychotropic therapeutic practices, including biofeedback, somatic therapy, and herbal and nutritional therapies. The memory-body connection does not in and of itself rationalize psychopharmaceutical intervention.

18. Kramer glosses this aspect of Tess's case in one brief sentence in the opening of his case study: "She was abused in childhood in the concrete physical and sexual senses which everyone understands as abuse" (1).

19. Common symptoms of serotonin depletion, one of the neurobiological effects of stress, can be treated with natural therapies as well as synthetic ones. Natural treatments, including light therapy, exercise, melatonin for insomnia, negative air ion treatments, and nutritional changes designed to adjust hormonal balances of insulin and glucagon to stabilize the brain's supply of glucose, have been used to replace or supplement prescribed drug treatments for depression and anxiety. See Dr. Michael Norden's *Beyond Prozac* (1995) for a review of the literature on natrual antidotes. Norden is a psychiatrist and professor who supports alternative and supplementary treatments for depression. Norden sees depression as a symptom of modern society brought on primarily by environmental stress in the form of alarm clocks that break natural sleep cycles, cars that make walking obsolete, sixty-hour work weeks that cause fatigue, natural light deprivation, recycled indoor air or polluted city air, and improper diet. Importantly, he does also acknowledge that childhood trauma can permanently damage a person's serotonin system in its developmental phase—which he theorizes to be the body's stress-coping system (17). Norden's book is an indispensable resource guide for alternative treatments of depression and anxiety. But Norden doesn't push the social-environmental connection far enough. For example, he discusses Dan White's case without even mentioning White's homophobia as a crucial determining factor in his murder of San Francisco Mayor George Moscone in 1978 (18). The point is that psychopharmacology should not be used to normalize the effects of a systematic flow of violences through the social body. On an individual level, one must struggle with the organic effects of depression and anxiety in whatever ways that one can make work for oneself, but pharmaceutical treatment alone can never and should never stand in the place of a conscious understanding of the social history of violence, and of one's own relation to that history, including one's lived memory of it, one's bodily experience with it, and one's affective response to it.

Works Cited

Acker, Kathy. "Dead Doll Humility." *Postmodern Culture*, 1, no. 1 (September 1990). World Wide Web http://lists.village.virginia.edu/pmc/

Arendt, Hannah. *On Violence*. New York: Harcourt, Brace, & World, 1969.

Armstrong, Louise. *And They Call It Help: The Psychiatric Policing of America's Children*. Reading, Mass.: Addison-Wesley, 1993.

Attali, Jacques. *Noise: The Political Economy of Music*. Trans. Brian Massumi. Minneapolis: University of Minnesota Press, 1985.

Barnouw, Erik. "The Case of the A-Bomb Footage." In *Transmissions*. Ed. Peter D'Agostino. New York: Tanam Press, 1985.

Bataille, Georges. *The Accursed Share: An Essay on General Economy, Volume 1*. Trans. Robert Hurley. New York: Zone Books, 1988.

Baudrillard, Jean. *In the Shadow of the Silent Majorities . . . or The End of the Social and Other Essays*. Trans. Paul Foss, Paul Patton, and John Johnson. New York: Semiotext(e), 1983.

Becraft, Carolyn H. "Women and the Military: Bureaucratic Policies and Politics." *Bureaucrat*, Fall 1989: 33–36.

Benjamin, Walter. *Illuminations*. Trans. Harry Zohn. New York: Schocken Books, 1978.

Bilton, Michael, and Kevin Sim. *Four Hours in My Lai*. New York: Penguin, 1992.

Boulègue, Jean. "'Feminization' and the French Military: An Anthropological Approach." Trans. Faris R. Kirkland. *Armed Forces & Society* 17.3 (1991): 343–62.

Boundas, Constantin, and Dorothea Olkowski, eds. *Gilles Deleuze and the Theater of Philosophy*. New York: Routledge, 1994.

Brady, Judith, ed. *1 in 3: Women with Cancer Confront an Epidemic*. Pittsburgh: Cleis Press, 1991.

Braidotti, Rosi. "Feminist Deleuzian Tracks; or, Metaphysics and Metabolism." In *Gilles Deleuze and the Theater of Philosophy*. Ed. Constantin Boundas and Dorothea Olkowski. New York: Routledge, 1994.

Breggin, Peter R., M.D. "Prozac Talks: An Interview with Peter Breggin." Interviewed by Gail Shepherd. *Red Herring*, 1, no. 1 (August 15, 1994): 15–17.

Breggin, Peter R., M.D., and Ginger Ross Breggin. *Talking Back to Prozac*. New York: St. Martin's Press, 1994.

Breggin, Peter R., M.D. *Toxic Psychiatry: Why Therapy, Empathy and Love Must Replace the Drugs, Electroshock and Biochemical Theories of the New Psychiatry*. New York: St. Martin's Press, 1991.

Briggs, Jimmie, and Kenneth Miller. "The Tiny Victims of Desert Storm." *Life* (November 1995): 45–62.

Bright, Susie. *Susie Sexpert's Lesbian Sex World*. Pittsburgh: Cleis Press, 1990.

———. *Susie Bright's Sexual Reality: A Virtual Sex World Reader*. Pittsburgh: Cleis Press, 1992.

Brownworth, Victoria. "Killer Lesbians." *Village Voice*, 37, no. 4 (October 13, 1992): 25.

Byram, Stephanie. "Cancer Destroys, Cancer Builds." Photographs by Charlee Brodsky. *Cultronix*, 1, no. 4 (April 1996). World Wide Web http://english-www.hss.cmj.edu/cultronix/

Califia, Pat. *Macho Sluts*. Boston: Alyson, 1988.

Canguilhem, Georges. *A Vital Rationalist: Selected Writings from Georges Canguilhem*. Ed. François Delaporte. New York: Zone Books, 1994.

Cartwright, Lisa. *Screening the Body: Tracing Medicine's Visual Culture*. Minneapolis: University of Minnesota Press, 1995.

Case, Sue-Ellen. "Tracking the Vampire." *differences: A Journal of Feminist Cultural Studies*, 5.2 (1991):1–20.

Center for Defense Information. *1995 Military Almanac*. Washington, D.C.: U.S. Government Printing Office, 1995.

Chandler, Raymond. *The Big Sleep*. New York: Ballantine Books, 1971.

Chibbaro, Lou, Jr. "ROTC Students Forced to Sign 'Inquisitorial' Affadavit." *Gay People's Chronicle*, December 18, 1992: 4.

Cohn, Carol. "Clean Bombs and Clean Language." In *Women, Militarism and War: Essays in History, Politics and Social Theory*. Ed. Jean Bethke Elshtain and Sheila Tobias. Savage, Md.: Rowman & Littlefield, 1990.

Cole, Jean Hascall. *Women Pilots of World War II*. Salt Lake City: University of Utah Press, 1992.

Copeland, Peter. "As Battle Ended, Burden Began for Celebrated Woman Warrior." *Rocky Mountain News*, June 30, 1991: 4.

Corea, Gena. *The Mother Machine: Reproductive Technology from Artificial Insemination to Artificial Wombs*. New York: Harper & Row, 1986.

Creet, Julia. "Daughter of the Movement: The Psychodynamics of Lesbian S/M Fantasy." *differences: A Journal of Feminist Cultural Studies*, 3.2 (1991): 135–59.

Crone, Hugh. *Chemicals and Society: A Guide to the New Chemical Age*. Cambridge: Cambridge University Press, 1986.

De Landa, Manuel. *War in the Age of Intelligent Machines*. New York: Zone Books, 1991.

———. "*War in the Age of Intelligent Machines*: An Interview with Manuel De Landa." Interviewed by Andrew Payne. *Public*, 6 (1992): 126–34.

Deleuze, Gilles. *Cinema 1: The Movement-Image*. Trans. Hugh Tomlinson and Barbara Habberjam. Minneapolis: University of Minnesota Press, 1986.

———. *Cinema 2: The Time-Image*. Trans. Hugh Tomlinson and Robert Galeta. Minneapolis: University of Minnesota Press, 1989.

———. *The Deleuze Reader*. Ed. Constantin Boundas. New York: Columbia University Press, 1993.

Deleuze, Gilles, and Félix Guattari. *Anti-Oedipus: Capitalism and Schizophrenia*. Trans. Robert Hurley, Mark Seem, and Helen Lane. Minneapolis: University of Minnesota Press, 1983.

———. *A Thousand Plateaus: Capitalism and Schizophrenia*. Trans. Brian Massumi. Minneapolis: University of Minnesota Press, 1987.

D'Emilio, John. *Sexual Politics, Sexual Communities: The Making of a Homosexual Minority in the United States, 1940–1970*. Chicago: University of Chicago Press, 1983.

Department of Defense. *Military Manpower Statistics: September 30, 1994*. Washington, D.C.: U.S. Government Printing Office, 1994.

Devlin, Polly. "Photography and Fashion." *Vogue Book of Fashion Photography, 1919–1979*. New York: Condé Nast Publications, 1979.

Dominiak, George. "Psychopharmacology of the Abused." In *Sexual Trauma and Psychopathology: Clinical Intervention with Adult Survivors*. Ed. George Dominiak and Shanti Shapiro. New York: Lexington Books, 1992.

Doyle, Edward, et al. *The Vietnam Experience: The Aftermath, 1975–85*. Boston: Boston Publishing, 1985.

Elshtain, Jean Bethke, ed. *Just War Theory*. New York: New York University Press, 1992.

Enloe, Cynthia. *Bananas, Beaches, and Bases: Making Feminist Sense of International Politics*. Berkeley: University of California Press, 1990.

———. "Home Fires: The Right to Fight, a Feminist Catch-22." *Ms.*, 4, no. 1 (July–August 1993): 84–87.

Environmental Protection Agency. *Toxic Release Inventory*. Washington, D.C. , 1992.

Epstein, Julia, and Kristina Straub. *Body Guards: The Cultural Politics of Gender Ambiguity*. New York: Routledge, 1991.

Epstein, Samuel. "Evaluation of the National Cancer Program and Proposed Reforms." *International Journal of Health Services*, 23, no. 1 (1993): 15–44.

Falk, F., et al. "Pesticides and PCB Residues in Human Breast Lipids and Their Relation to Breast Cancer." *Archives of Environmental Health*, 47 (1992): 143–46.

Faludi, Susan. *Backlash: The Undeclared War against American Women*. New York: Doubleday, 1991.

Foucault, Michel. *Discipline and Punish: The Birth of the Prison*. Trans. Alan Sheridan. New York: Vintage Books, 1979.

———. *The History of Sexuality, Volume 1*. New York: Vintage Books, 1980.

Freeman, Walter Jackson, and James Watts. *Psychosurgery in the Treatment of Mental Disorders*. 2nd ed. Springfield, Ill.: Charles C. Thomas, 1950.

Gilmartin, Patricia A. "Senate Endorses New SDI Plan, Wider Role for Women in Combat." *Aviation Week & Space Technology*, August 5, 1991: 24.

Girard, René. *Violence and the Sacred*. Trans. Patrick Gregory. Baltimore: Johns Hopkins University Press, 1977.

Grace, Della. *Love Bites*. London: GMP, 1991.

"The Great and Growing Pilot Shortage" (editorial). *Far Eastern Economic Review*, February 4, 1988: 58–61.

Greenhouse, Linda. "High Court Rules 1871 Klan Act Cannot Stop Abortion Blockades." *New York Times*, January 14, 1993: A-1.

Gross, Andrea. "Up Front: Our Women at War." *Ladies Home Journal*, April 1991: 51–52.

Grosz, Elizabeth. "A Thousand Tiny Sexes: Feminism and Rhizomatics." In *Gilles Deleuze and the Theater of Philosophy*. Ed. Constantin Boundas and Dorothea Olkowski. New York: Routledge, 1994.

Guattari, Félix. *Molecular Revolution: Psychiatry and Politics*. Trans. Rosemary Sheed. New York: Penguin Books, 1984.

Habermas, Jürgen. *The Structural Transformation of the Public Sphere: An Inquiry into a Category of Bourgeois Society*. Trans. Thomas Burger. Cambridge, Mass.: MIT Press, 1992.

Hammett, Dashiell. *The Continental Op*. New York: Vintage Books, 1975.

Handel, Neal, M.D. "Current Status of Breast Reconstruction after Mastectomy." *Oncology*, 5, no. 11 (November 1991): 73–84.

Haraway, Donna. *Primate Visions: Gender, Race, and Nature in the World of Modern Science*. New York: Routledge, 1989.

———. *Simians, Cyborgs, and Women: The Reinvention of Nature*. New York: Routledge, 1991.

Hardt, Michael. *Gilles Deleuze: An Apprenticeship in Philosophy*. Minneapolis: University of Minnesota Press, 1993.

Harrison, Kathryn. *Exposure*. New York: Random House, 1993.

Herman, Judith. *Father-Daughter Incest*. Cambridge, Mass.: Harvard University Press, 1981.

———. *Trauma and Recovery*. New York: HarperCollins, 1992.

Hess, Elizabeth. "Hypnotic Constructions of Reality in Trauma and Treatment." In *Sexual Trauma and Psychopathology: Clinical Intervention with Adult Survivors*. Ed. George Dominiak and Shanti Shapiro. New York: Lexington Books, 1992.

Hirano, Kyoko. *Mr. Smith Goes to Tokyo: Japanese Cinema under the American Occupation, 1945–1952*. Washington, D.C.: Smithsonian Institution Press, 1992.

Holzer, Jenny. *The Venice Installation*. Buffalo, N.Y.: Albright-Knox Art Gallery, 1990.

hooks, bell. *Ain't I a Woman: Black Women and Feminism*. Boston: South End Press, 1981.

Ide, Arthur. *Abortion Handbook: The History, Legal Progress, Practice and Psychology of Abortion*. Las Colinas, Texas: Liberal Press, 1986.

Irigaray, Luce. *This Sex Which Is Not One*. Trans. Catherine Porter. Ithaca, N.Y.: Cornell University Press, 1985.

Itzen, Catherine. "'Entertainment for Men': What It Is and What It Means." In *Pornography: Women, Violence and Civil Liberties*. Ed. Catherine Izten. New York: Oxford University Press, 1992.

Jardine, Alice. *Gynesis: Configurations of Woman and Modernity*. Ithaca, N.Y.: Cornell University Press, 1985.

Johnson, Barbara. *A World of Difference*. Baltimore: The Johns Hopkins University Press, 1987.

Jones, Kathleen. "Dividing the Ranks: Women and the Draft." In *Women, Militarism and War*. Ed. Jean Bethke Elshtain and Sheila Tobias. Savage, Md.: Rowman & Littlefield, 1990.

Kaysen, Susanna. *Girl, Interrupted*. New York: Vintage Books, 1993.

Kaw Eugenia. "Medicalization of Racial Features: Asian American Women and Cosmetic Surgery." *Medical Anthropology Quarterly: International Journal for the Analysis of Health*, 7, no. 1 (March 1993): 74–89.

Kittler, Friedrich. "Media Wars: Trenches, Lightning, Stars." *1–800*, 1, no. 1 (1989): 3–9.

Kramer, Peter. *Listening to Prozac*. New York: Viking, 1993.

Kristeva, Julia. "Ellipsis on Dread and the Specular Seduction." In *Narrative, Apparatus, Ideology*. Ed Philip Rosen. New York: Columbia University Press, 1986.

———. *Powers of Horror: An Essay on Abjection*. Trans. Leon Roudiez. New York: Columbia University Press, 1982.

———. *Tales of Love*. Trans. Leon S. Roudiez. New York: Columbia University Press, 1987.

Lacan, Jacques. *Seminar III: The Psychoses*. New York: W. W. Norton, 1993.

Laplanche, Jean and J.-B. Pontalis. *The Language of Psycho-Analysis*. Trans. Donald Nicholson-Smith. New York: W. W. Norton, 1973.

Lopez, Ana. "The Melodrama in Latin America: Films, Telenovelas, and the Currency of a Popular Form." In *Imitations of Life: A Reader on Film and Television Melodrama*. Ed. Marcia Landy. Detroit: Wayne State University Press, 1991.

Lorde, Audre. *Zami, A New Spelling of My Name*. Watertown, Mass.: Persephone Press, 1982.

Lyotard, Jean-Francois. *The Postmodern Condition*. Trans. Geoff Bennington and Brian Massumi. Minneapolis: University of Minnesota Press, 1986.

MacCannell, Dean. "Faking It: Comment on Face-Work in Pornography." *The American Journal of Semiotics*, 6, no. 4 (1989): 153–74.

MacNamara, Mark. "The Kiss-And-Kill Spree." *Vanity Fair*, September 1991: 90, 106.

Massumi, Brian. *A User's Guide to Capitalism and Schizophrenia: Deviations from Deleuze and Guattari*. Cambridge, Mass.: MIT Press, 1992.

The Merck Index, 11th Edition. Rahway, N.J.: Merck and Co., 1989.

Merrell, Kathy. "Designing Women." *Allure*. January 1995.

Millett, Kate. *The Looney-Bin Trip*. New York: Simon and Schuster, 1990.

Moore, Brenda I. "African-American Women in the U.S. Military." *Armed Forces & Society*, 17.3 (1991): 363–84.

Morrison, Toni. *The Bluest Eye*. New York: Washington Square Press, 1970.

Morse, Margaret. "What Do Cyborgs Eat? Oral Logic in an Information Society." In *Culture on the Brink: Ideologies of Technology*. Ed. Gretchen Bender and Timothy Druckrey. Seattle: Bay Press, 1994.

National Cancer Institute. *Cancer Statistics Review 1973–1988*. Bethesda, Md.: NIH Publication No. 91–2789, 1991.

Norden, Michael, M.D. *Beyond Prozac: Brain-Toxic Lifestyles, Natural Antidotes and New Generation Antidepressants*. New York: HarperCollins, 1995.

Office of the Inspector General, Department of Defense. *The Tailhook Report: The Official Inquiry into the Events of Tailhook '91*. New York: St. Martin's Press, 1993.

Ong, Walter. *Orality and Literacy: The Technologizing of the Word*. New York: Routledge, 1982.

Overall, Christine, ed. *The Future of Human Reproduction*. Ontario: Women's Press, 1989.

Palmer, Elizabeth. "Senate Debates Rights, Role of Women Warriors." *Congressional Quarterly Weekly Report*, June 22, 1991: 1687.

Pontoni, Martha. "Woman Kills Lover." *Gay People's Chronicle* (Cleveland), 8, no. 2, August 21, 1992: 2.

Popper, Frank. *Art of the Electronic Age*. Singapore: Thames and Hudson, 1993.

Randolph, Laura B. "The Untold Story of Black Women in the Gulf War." *Ebony*, September 1991: 100–107.

Rhymer, Russ. *Genie: An Abused Child's Flight from Silence*. New York: HarperCollins, 1993.

Rickels, Laurence. *Aberrations of Mourning: Writing on German Crypts*. Detroit: Wayne State University Press, 1988.

Rimer, Sara. "With Millions Taking Prozac, a Legal Drug Culture Arises." *New York Times*, July 18, 1992: B–1.

Rodman, Hyman, Betty Sarvis, and Joy Bonar. *The Abortion Question*. New York: Columbia University Press, 1987.

Ronell, Avital. *Finitude's Score: Essays for the End of the Millennium*. Lincoln: University of Nebraska Press, 1994.

———. "Haunted TV: Rodney King/Video/Trauma." *Artforum*, September 1992: 71–74.

———. *The Telephone Book: Technology, Schizophrenia, Electric Speech*. Lincoln: University of Nebraska Press, 1989.

SAMOIS. *Coming to Power: Writings and Graphics on Lesbian S/M*. Boston: Alyson, 1987.

Scarry, Elaine. "The Merging of Bodies and Artifacts in the Social Contract." In *Culture on the Brink: Ideologies of Technology*." Ed. Gretchen Bender and Timothy Druckrey. Seattle: Bay Press, 1994.

Schivelbusch, Wolfgang. *Disenchanted Night: The Industrialization of Light in the Nineteenth Century*. Trans. Angela Davies. Berkeley: University of California Press, 1988.

———. *The Railway Journey: The Industrialization of Time and Space in the Nineteenth Century*. Berkeley: University of California Press, 1986.

Schultze, Charles, Edward Fried, Alice Rivlin, Nancy Teeters. *Setting National Priorities: The 1973 Budget*. Washington, D.C.: The Brookings Institution, 1972.

Sechehaye, Marguerite. *Autobiography of a Schizophrenic Girl*. New York: New American Library, 1970.

Sedgwick, Eve Kosofsky. "Queer Performativity: Henry James' *The Art of the Novel*." *Gay/Lesbian Quarterly*, 1, no. 1 (1993): 1–16.

Shapiro, Shanti. "Suicidality and the Sequelae of Childhood Victimization." In *Sexual Trauma and Psychopathology: Clinical Intervention with Adult Survivors*. Ed. George Dominiak and Shanti Shapiro. New York: Lexington Books, 1992.

Sloterdijk, Peter. *Critique of Cynical Reason*. Trans. Michael Eldred. Minneapolis: University of Minnesota Press, 1987.

Sontag, Susan. "Notes on Camp." In *A Susan Sontag Reader*. New York: Farrar, Straus, Giroux, 1982.

Spillane, Mickey. *I the Jury*. New York: New American Library, 1954.

Stewart, Susan. "The Marquis de Meese." *Critical Inquiry*, 15.1 (1988): 162–93.

Stiehm, Judith Hicks. *Arms and the Enlisted Woman*. Philadelphia: Temple University Press, 1989.

Stone, Elizabeth. "The Personality Pill." *Mirabella* (June 1993): 86–92.

Stone, Sandy. "The Empire Strikes Back: A Posttranssexual Manifesto." In *Body Guards*. Ed. Julia Epstein and Kristina Straub. New York: Routledge, 1991.

Swerdlow, Amy. "Motherhood and the Subversion of the Military State: Women's Strike for Peace Confronts the House Committee on Un-American Activities." In *Women, Militarism, and War: Essays in History, Politics, and Social Theory*. Ed. Jean Bethke Elshtain and Sheila Tobias. Savage, Md.: Rowan & Littlefield, 1990.

Taussig, Michael. *The Nervous System*. New York: Routledge, 1992.

———. *Shamanism, Colonialism, and the Wildman: A Study in Terror and Healing*. Chicago: University of Chicago Press, 1987.

Tribe, Laurence. *Abortion: The Clash of Absolutes*. New York: W. W. Norton, 1992.

Trinh, T. Minh-Ha. *Woman, Native, Other: Writing Postcoloniality and Feminism*. Bloomington: Indiana University Press, 1989.

United Nations International Children's Emergency Fund. *The State of the World's Children*. Oxford: Oxford University Press, 1996.

U.S. Bureau of the Census. *Statistical Abstract of the United States: 1995*. (115th ed.) Washington, D.C.: U.S. Bureau of the Census, 1995.

U.S. Department of Health and Human Services. *1992 Ambulatory Medical Care Survey*. CD-ROM Series, 13, no. 4. ("Ambulatory Care, Psychiatric Treatment.") Hyattsville, Md.: National Center for Health Statistics, 1995.

Virilio, Paul. *Popular Defense and Ecological Struggles*. New York: Autonomedia, 1990.

Wasserman, M., et al. "Organochlorine Compounds in Neoplastic and Adjacent Apparently Normal Breast Tissue." *Bulletin on Environmental Contaminants and Toxicology*, (1976): 15, 478–84.

Williams, Donna. *Nobody, Nowhere: The Extraordinary Autobiography of an Autistic*. New York: Times Books, 1992.

Willis, Rudy. *Total War and Twentieth Century Higher Learning Universities of the Western World in the First and Second World Wars*. Cranbury, N.J.: Fairleigh Dickinson University Press, 1991.

Wittig, Monique. *The Straight Mind*. Boston: Beacon Press, 1992.

Women in Combat: Report to the President. Presidential Commission on the Assignment of Women in the Armed Forces. Washington, D.C.: Brassey's, 1993.

Yarbrough, Jeff. "RuPaul: The Man Behind the Mask." *The Advocate*, no. 661/662 (August 23, 1994): 64–72.

Zapatista press release. "Subcommander Marcos Is More Than Just Gay." *Monthly Review*, 46, no. 4 (1994): 1.

Index

Camilla Griggers holds an endowed chair in women's studies in
the Division of Humanities at Carlow College.
She is a founding editor of the e-journal *Cultronix* on the World Wide Web and
producer of the video *Alienations of the Mother Tongue*.